Markham
Shaping a Destiny

*P*roduced in cooperation with the
Markham Board of Trade

Markham
Shaping a Destiny

Jerry Amernic *Editorial Coordinator*

Marianne Tefft *Profile Coordinator*

Benjamin Rondel *Chief Photographer*

Markham: Shaping a Destiny
Produced in cooperation with the
Markham Board of Trade
3780 14th Avenue, Suite 210
Markham, Ontario L3R 9Y5
(905) 474-0730
www.markhamboard.com

Editorial Coordinator: Jerry Amernic
Profile Coordinator: Marianne Tefft
Chief Photographer: Benjamin Rondel

Community Communications, Inc.
Publishers: Ronald P. Beers and James E. Turner

Staff for *Markham: Shaping a Destiny*
Publisher's Sales Associate: C. Brian Rhodes
Executive Editor: James E. Turner
Managing Editor: Linda Moeller Pegram
Design Director: Camille Leonard
Designer: Summer Barrett
Photo Editors: Summer Barrett and Linda M. Pegram
Production Manager: Cindy Lovett
Editorial Assistants: Robin Davies and Jarrod Stiff
Contract Manager: Katrina Williams
Sales Assistant: Annette R. Lozier
Proofreader: Wynona B. Hall
Accounting Services: Sara Ann Turner
Printing Production: Frank Rosenberg/GSAmerica

Community Communications, Inc.
Montgomery, Alabama

James E. Turner, Chairman of the Board
Ronald P. Beers, President
Daniel S. Chambliss, Vice President

© 1998 Community Communications
All Rights Reserved
Published 1998
Printed in Canada
First Edition
Library of Congress Catalog Number: 98-38584
ISBN: 1-885352-78-6

Every effort has been made to ensure the accuracy of the information herein. However, the authors and Community Communications are not responsible for any errors or omissions which might have occurred.

Part I

Foreword Page 7
Preface Page 9

Chapter One

A History of Surpassing Expectations
Page 10

Chapter Two

**Preserving a Sense of Place:
Markham's Neighbourhoods**
by Andy Shaw
Page 18

Chapter Three

**Creating an Atmosphere
for Business**
Page 28

Chapter Four

Establishing High-Tech Connections
by David Menzies
Page 36

Chapter Five

**Turning Progress into Prosperity:
Markham's Chinese Community**
Page 42

Chapter Six

Shaping the Spirit of Markham: Arts & Culture
Page 48

Chapter Seven

A Legacy of Caring: Health Care & Education
Page 54

Part II

Bibliography Page 100
Acknowledgements Page 100
Enterprise Index Page 101
Index Page 102

Chapter Eight

The Business Community
Page 62

*Markham Board of Trade 64-65
Craig Riley's Markville Lincoln Mercury 66-67
TD Financial Group 68
Ceridian Canada Ltd. 69
Town of Markham 70-71
BridgeStreet Accommodations 72
V.V. DeMarco Properties, Limited 73
JJ Barnicke Limited 74
Toronto Airways Ltd. 75*

Chapter Nine

High Technology
Page 76

*IBM Canada Ltd. 78-79
Comtronic Computers 80
Technica House Canada Inc. 81
GE Multilin 82-83
Humphrey Fluid Power Limited 84-85
Delfour Corporation 86-87
Computron Systems 88
InSystems Technologies 89
Eprom Inc. 90
Jaba System Inc. 91*

Chapter Ten

Manufacturing & Distribution
Page 92

*Shepherd Products Inc. 94-95
Jannex Enterprises Ltd. 96
Automated Systems Incorporated 97
BT Canada Ltd. 98
Framatome Connectors International 99*

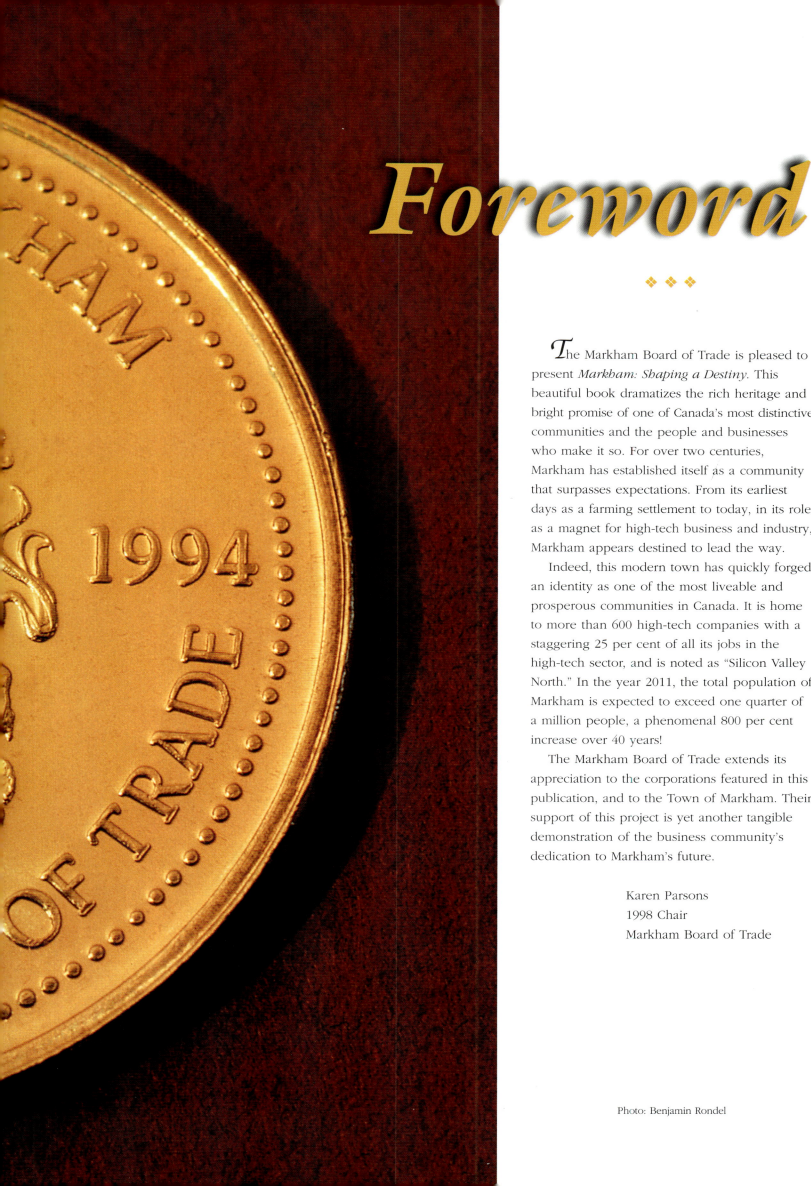

Foreword

✦✦✦

*T*he Markham Board of Trade is pleased to present *Markham: Shaping a Destiny*. This beautiful book dramatizes the rich heritage and bright promise of one of Canada's most distinctive communities and the people and businesses who make it so. For over two centuries, Markham has established itself as a community that surpasses expectations. From its earliest days as a farming settlement to today, in its role as a magnet for high-tech business and industry, Markham appears destined to lead the way.

Indeed, this modern town has quickly forged an identity as one of the most liveable and prosperous communities in Canada. It is home to more than 600 high-tech companies with a staggering 25 per cent of all its jobs in the high-tech sector, and is noted as "Silicon Valley North." In the year 2011, the total population of Markham is expected to exceed one quarter of a million people, a phenomenal 800 per cent increase over 40 years!

The Markham Board of Trade extends its appreciation to the corporations featured in this publication, and to the Town of Markham. Their support of this project is yet another tangible demonstration of the business community's dedication to Markham's future.

Karen Parsons
1998 Chair
Markham Board of Trade

Photo: Benjamin Rondel

Preface

❖ ❖ ❖

I first moved to the east end of what was Metropolitan Toronto back in 1974. The area to the east and north of Canada's biggest city was an attraction because of its many beautiful and natural surroundings. Indeed, it was very easy for me to forget that I was next door to a huge metropolis. And I liked that. Markham, in particular, has been a special place. It has experienced growth that is nothing short of spectacular. In fact, since the time I moved to the east end, Markham might just be the fastest growing municipality in all of Canada.

Incredibly, in a relatively short period of time, what was once a generally rural area has become a leading centre of business, commerce and high technology. Markham today is an engine of economic growth, a major player on the Canadian scene. At the same time, however, its villages have managed to retain an aura of small-town friendliness and hospitality which is often swallowed up and lost in modern, sprawling cities. Markham has also retained a bountiful inventory of parks, ravines and natural settings.

Preparing this book has been a real pleasure as it got me in touch with those elements that make a town truly successful. The people of Markham should be very proud of the community they have built. I hope this book will give you an insight into a very special municipality. It's one that really works. On second thought, why don't you come and find out for yourself? You just might stay.

Jerry Amernic

Photo: Benjamin Rondel

Part I

Chapter One

A History of Surpassing Expectations

❖ ❖ ❖

For over two centuries, Markham has established itself as a community that surpasses expectations. From its earliest days as a farming settlement, when it earned a reputation for outstanding soil, possibly the finest in Upper Canada, to today, in its role as a magnet for high-tech business and industry, Markham appears destined to lead the way. Indeed, the modern town of Markham has quickly forged an identity as one of the most liveable and prosperous communities in Canada.

The vibrant entrepreneurial spirit of Markham began with its very first developer—William Berczy. Responding to a request for quality European settlers from Ontario's first Lieutenant-Governor, John Graves Simcoe, Berczy obtained 64,000 acres of land and named the new settlement after William Markham, England's Archbishop of York and friend of the Simcoe family. The immediate area was surveyed in 1793 and 1794 and laid out in 10 concessions running north and south from Yonge Street in the west to the Pickering town line in the east. Each concession was then divided into 200-acre lots.

Markham's first European inhabitants, some 200 strong, spent the winter of 1794-95 in log houses in an uncleared forest. Berczy wanted to establish a thriving community, but the early settlers suffered disease and a bad crop. Still, the land held a fascination for settlers from the United Kingdom, and they kept coming. The first inhabitants of what is now Markham, however, were Iroquois tribes who lived in the region a thousand years ago. Later, during the 15th and 16th centuries, Native Americans were active in the fur trade along with early English and French explorers.

Photo: Benjamin Rondel

The German Berczy was a man unaccustomed to failure. He cleared the banks of the Rouge River and several water mills were then established. Many of the original 200-acre lots were subdivided among the offspring of the first settlers, and soon the average acreage in Markham was 100 acres. The first cash crop was probably potash, the ash that remained after trees were burned to clear the land.

Yonge Street was central to the fledgling communities established north of York, or Toronto. The street was used as a fur trade artery to the north and in times of conflict, as in the War of 1812, to transport military supplies. Once clearings were made for the roadway, villages began to form.

The village of Thornhill, named after local merchant Benjamin Thorne, was at first an important milling centre, but soon had to yield the role to the much larger community of York. By 1840, Thornhill boasted four churches, two schools, a post office, stagecoach service and a toll gate.

The villages depended on agriculture. By the mid 1800s, the main cash crops were wheat and barley, while local businesses provided families with everything from cloth and shoes to furniture and farm equipment. Before long the farms began to gain renown.

In 1844, the *British American Cultivator* reported this about the 500 to 600 cultivated farms in the township of Markham: "[They are] so perfectly cleared that scarcely a stump can be seen in tracts of some miles in extent, and which land cannot be excelled in quality. We would not be much surprised if the intelligent and wealthy farmers of Markham would continue to persevere in their laudable efforts to advance, strengthen and establish the character of their noble calling. . . ."

And a noble calling it was. In the 1860s new machines like the reaper and binder further enhanced the productivity of the farmers. In 1871, the *County of York Directory* referred to Markham as "one of the finest wheat growing townships in the Dominion." Later advances brought even more prosperity to the region as steam power took over from horses; steam became the fuel for threshing, establishing a career for many Markham families.

James L. Langstaff was an early area physician whose legacy includes both a son and a grandson who became local doctors. A wing of York Central Hospital, in York, Ontario, was named in honour of the family.
Photo courtesy Markham District Historical Museum.

While agriculture was a staple of the growing communities, the local economies prospered with new transportation routes. The waterways had served the original inhabitants adequately, but roads were needed to connect the villages to Toronto in the south as well as to outlying areas. Some of the early roads were corduroy roads—tree trunks laid down side by side—and travelling them was anything but a smooth experience.

The Mill Road, which ran off Yonge Street to the settlement of German Mills and which was later renamed the Pomona Plank Road, was, in 1864, the township's first "macadam" road. Its construction involved placing a bed of large rocks at the base and then covering that up with broken stone. But macadamizing was costly, so plank roads proved more popular, and in 1852 the Markham and Scarborough Plank Company was established.

Of course, Yonge Street was the most vital road of all. The community of Richmond Hill to the north grew up along this artery, and by the turn of the century could boast of five hotels and three liquor stores, all on a one-and-a-half-mile stretch of Yonge Street. Local businesses in Richmond Hill also included the likes of tailors, barber shops, blacksmiths, tinsmiths and slaughterhouses.

Markham and its neighboring communities embrace the future, while preserving the unique traces of the past. Here, at the old planing mill in Unionville, visitors are invited to step back in time to when the area buzzed with the sound of more than 80 water-driven sawmills. Photo: Benjamin Rondel.

12 Shaping A Destiny

By the mid-19th century the railways became the lifeblood of such communities. The Ontario Simcoe and Huron Railway came to Yonge Street in 1853, while the eastern section of the township was later served by the Ontario and Quebec Railway. The Toronto and Nipissing Railway was formed in 1868, and it, too, was instrumental in the growth of the township of Markham. Then came an electric railway system; by 1899 the Metropolitan Radial Railway was completing five trips a day along Yonge Street, connecting the township to Toronto.

Throughout the 1800s, the villages were subject to calamity in the form of disease. In a cholera epidemic of 1832 a single family lost eight children, and their stark row of graves still stands in the old Lutheran cemetery in Buttonville. There were outbreaks of diphtheria and smallpox, and in the early 1900s a wave of influenza and later polio.

Such horrors kept physicians of the day busy, including a doctor named James L. Langstaff. He first practised in Unionville and then moved to Richmond Hill. His son Rolph, born in 1869, continued the tradition along with his wife, Lillian, and their practice became well-known in the community. Rolph Langstaff once delivered five babies in 24 hours, all of them born in farmhouses, and the total fee for his work was a paltry $20. For 25 years he was Richmond Hill's Medical Officer of Health, and his son James became a doctor as well. After 37 years of practise, James Langstaff retired in 1973, and one year later the addition of the 274-bed Langstaff Wing of York Central Hospital was named to honour this unique family.

The community of Unionville had been a mere hamlet with a population of 500 people at the turn of the century. Indeed, there were dressmakers, carpenters, cabinetmakers, blacksmiths, tailors, a miller, and at least one harness shop. Stouffville, on the other hand, was already a bustling village and a marketplace for farmers from the adjacent townships of Markham, Whitchurch, Uxbridge and Pickering.

Meanwhile, Markham Village, which began to thrive along the artery of Markham Road, or Highway 48, boasted 950 residents with four wagon and carriage manufacturing enterprises, a large woollen mill, two grist mills, three blacksmiths and three hotels. It also had two newspapers—the *Markham Economist*, which had been published since 1856, and the *Markham Sun*, which had been around since 1881. In 1915, the two merged.

What's key about these Markham-area communities is that they were all distinct, independent settlements in their own right and not mere bedroom communities of the big city to the south; in fact, Markham was a crossroads for the entire area.

In those days, washouts of dams were a frequent problem. On April 25, 1900, heavy rains raised water levels on the mill ponds of the Rouge River, and dams at Almira, Unionville and Dickinson Hill were all destroyed. In 1913, after Milne Dam in Markham Village was washed out for the third time, a concrete dam was built, and today this area is the site of a popular 40-hectare park.

As with most communities across Canada, the villages of Markham felt the effects of war. First it was the Boer War, which broke out in 1899 and which sent many Canadians to South Africa to assist Great Britain. But a far more urgent war knocked on Markham's door in 1914. During this time, a recruiting station was set up right in the heart of Markham. Local men served in such units as the Canadian Field Artillery, Army Medical Corps, Canadian Mounted

Candlemaking is just one of many pioneer demonstrations held at the annual Markham Museum Village Heritage Day.
Photo: Benjamin Rondel.

Rifles, and Royal Flying Corps. In fact, the family of air ace Billy Bishop, Canada's first airman to win the Victoria Cross, lived in Markham.

In 1918, many of Markham's farmers joined a mass rally in Toronto to protest the Military Service Act, which made the enlistment of farmers' sons mandatory, but this, of course, was crucial to the war effort. Improved mechanization was the only answer to the sudden shortage of manpower on the farms, and soon the grain combines brought a quick end to the threshing era.

When the conflict was finally over, more than 6,000 people met at the Markham Fair Grounds to honour the soldiers who had served in the Great War. In the years that immediately followed, Markham knew prosperity. All Canada was booming and few people believed it would ever slow down. However, a huge storm hit Markham in April, 1929, and perhaps it was a sign of things to come; the Rouge River overflowed and destroyed all of the mills. Six months later the stock market crashed.

In Markham, things went from bad to worse. In a single month in 1933, relief payments in the area equaled the total for all of 1931. This was the "dirty thirties" and for prosperous Markham it was a bitter pill, as the local communities had known only prosperous times for over a hundred years. Many farmers were able to grow enough to feed their families, but professionals such as doctors and dentists often had to be paid with food, instead of cash.

Then came the Second World War and everything changed. Suddenly all of Canada's economy was geared to the war effort. In Markham Township, more than 500 men and women joined the Canadian Armed Forces. By war's end, the villages of Markham, Unionville and Thornhill found themselves fulfilling their new roles as "bedroom communities" of Toronto.

In 1950 Markham Township celebrated its centennial with a parade and festivities in Markham Village and on the old Markham Fair Grounds. In the decade that followed, thousands of people came to Canada from the British Isles and Europe, and Markham was well on its way to becoming one of the most affluent places to live in all of Canada.

But every once in a while Mother Nature would remind the residents of their mortality. On October 15, 1954, Hurricane Hazel, the storm of the century, hit, and all the rivers in the Toronto area overflowed their banks. The Canadian National Railway's evening passenger train from Toronto was derailed by a washout just north of Markham Village, and within a few hours Markham Village was completely cut off from Toronto. A total of some 11 bridges were destroyed. But, as always, the people of Markham managed to come together. Engineers of the Second Canadian Field Regiment, with help from the employees of Markham Township, quickly constructed a Bailey bridge to replace the Pomona Mills bridge in Thornhill. Bailey bridges were also built in

Milne's Pond and Grist Mill, circa 1890. Photo courtesy Markham District Historical Museum.

In 1954, in the aftermath of Hurricane Hazel, all of the rivers in the Toronto area overflowed, causing this train derailment just north of Markham.
Photo courtesy Markham District Historical Museum.

Unionville and at Cedar Grove on the Markham-Scarborough town line.

In the 1950s speculators bought much of the land in Markham, and the entire area underwent rapid development. As fewer and fewer people were needed as farmers, many in Markham's farming community continued working at enterprises related to agriculture: market gardening, vegetable farming, sod farms and nurseries and fruit-and-vegetable businesses.

The official designation of "village" was finally lost in 1970, when Unionville and the village of Markham rejoined the township of Markham to become the town of Markham, which took in all property east of Yonge Street. Incredible growth and development followed; in an eight-year span between 1971 and 1979, the total tax assessment of Markham actually doubled!

Markham became one of the fastest growing municipalities in Canada. Located just 30 minutes by car from downtown Toronto, it emerged as a leading centre that combined an urban lifestyle with a strong sense of community. Computer industry giants such as IBM and later Apple relocated their Canadian head offices here, and Markham quickly became the place for high technology. The business community was largely concentrated in the electronic, computer and financial service sectors, and Markham flourished as never before. In the last quarter of the 20th century, Markham consistently ranked as one of Canada's top municipalities in terms of average household income.

Still, the notion of village remains, and it is indeed a tribute to Markham that such places as the old Main Street in Markham Village have been spruced up like they used to be, if for no other reason than to remind the residents of their past. It's just an example of one of the qualities that make this community a wonderful place to live.

Traditionally, the people of Markham have looked after their communities with an eye toward preserving the best elements of the past, as illustrated in these Unionville scenes. Photos: Benjamin Rondel.

*At the Markham Museum Village, visitors can witness many of the sights and sounds of pioneer life in the villages.
Photos: Benjamin Rondel.*

Chapter Two

Preserving a Sense of Place

❖ ❖ ❖

Markham's Neighbourhoods

Nature has been kind to Markham. In fact, it's almost as if God took special care when peeling back the Wisconsin glacier covering the area some 13,000 years ago. To this day, the riches left by the retreating ice field nurture the diverse and well-cared-for neighbourhoods of the four villages and six hamlets where most of the residents live. Guarding them all, along the full length of Markham's still rural north flank, stands the glacial-deposited Oak Ridges Moraine. From its nearly 400-metre heights, rivers and creeks tumble southward to Lake Ontario. En route, the thicketed ravines of the Don, Rouge and Little Rouge Rivers, not to mention Duffin's and Petticoat Creeks, segment the undulating plain of fertile glacial till that forms the rest of Markham.

For more than 200 years, those waterways and soils have sustained Markham life. A little over a century ago, the town's early neighbourhoods buzzed with the sounds of more than 80 water-driven sawmills. The mills helped clear the way for the farms which still thrive today in Markham's north and east. Now, with the town's original forest cover cut back to isolated wood lots, the sawmills are forever silenced. But the waters remain. Dammed up into placid ponds, they sparkle at the centre of the town's major parklands. In all, 200 carefully tended parks separate and civilize the neighbourhoods of Markham's now thickly populated villages.

Photo: Benjamin Rondel

Whether you stroll through neighbourhoods of the large and luxurious homes of Unionville, by high-rise apartments of Thornhill, past town houses of Milliken Mills, or among turn-of-the-century clapboard homes in the original village of Markham itself, the town's natural history calls out to you. Doves coo from the overhead wires, and at last count, they, along with northern cardinals, song sparrows, blue jays, red robins and goldfinches, were among the 77 bird species observed in and about Markham's backyards.

Their flocks mingle in even greater numbers (along with at least 12 kinds of mammals, including white-tailed deer) amidst the rolling meadows of the town's north end below the Whitchurch-Stouffville town line. Here, Markham's tasteful neighbourhoods of country estates form a serene oasis, at least until the first weekend of October, when the Markham Fair bursts joyously upon the fall air as it has every year since the 1850s.

From the Markham Fair Grounds in the north, forming an arc to Markham's boundary with the town of Pickering in the southeast, is a string of hamlets. The neighbourhoods of Victoria Square, Almira, Dickinson Hill, Box Grove, Locust Hill and Cedar Grove all recall Markham's human heritage. They owe their origins to a grist mill, an inn, a church or a post office that once served the surrounding farms. With many of these buildings still standing today, the hamlets help anchor Markham to its past.

Now the hamlets politely interrupt Markham's sweep of luxuriant cornfields, productive pastures and some 14 verdant golf and country clubs. They were all first cleared by the sweat of long-serving pioneers.

"People in the past didn't just move in and move out; they became fixtures. You knew who everyone was," recalled long-time Markham observer D. Evelyn "Lynn" Hughes a few years before her death in 1996. "I think people come out here still to get that feeling. They want what we had way back then—being close to a community that cares."

Lynn Hughes became a pioneer farmer in her own right when she and her husband, Dean, moved from the city and bought Briarwood Farms in the heart of Markham in 1945. (Dean Hughes, a writer, immortalized the mythical Markham "Craig" family farm in a long-running series on national CBC radio.) Together, they bore witness to the town's remarkable growth. When they moved at the end of the Second World War, Markham's population stood at just over 7,000. By the early 1900s Markham's neighbourhoods housed more than 150,000 people, and in the year 2011, town planners predict a count of over 260,000.

Nature has been kind to Markham, and the town's residents in turn have taken a proactive stance in protecting and preserving their environment, as evidenced by the area's many parks and green spaces. Photo: Benjamin Rondel.

The building of the north-south Highway 404 that forms the longest portion of Markham's western boundary with the town of Richmond Hill and the widening of Markham's main east-west artery, Highway 7, opened the gates not only to Toronto's overflow but to the housing developers who quickly followed.

First, the neighbourhoods of Thornhill in Markham's southwest corner, and then Milliken Mills along the town's southern border with the former city of Scarborough began to fill. People came looking for a quality of life that was not available in the big city. They also moved in along Highway 7, filling up the space between Unionville and Markham Village with suburbs.

Serene vistas such as this one at Toogood Pond provide ample opportunities for relaxation and recreation. Photo: Benjamin Rondel.

20 Shaping A Destiny

All this has made Markham one of Canada's fastest growing communities.

Yet, typical of the town, Markham's political leaders have managed this spectacular expansion with care. By balancing industrial and residential tax bases, Markham town council has attracted high-paying technology and other "clean" industries and, at the same time, preserved the essentially rural nature of its core neighbourhoods.

However, preserving the past for the future sometimes takes on rather unneighbourly confrontation. In 1968, Unionville's politicians deemed that growth was a universal good and proposed to widen the village's main street to four lanes. This would encourage more traffic, provide greater shopping convenience and stimulate Unionville's build-up. And, oh yes, a few historical buildings would have to come down in the name of progress.

Well, it should come as no surprise that the people of Unionville rejected this plan. The local heritage society stood firm and the street wideners retreated. Now, Unionville's Main Street is a two-lane delight of refurbished houses, stables, inns, a blacksmith's shop and a fire hall. Their owners have lovingly turned them into chic clothing boutiques, antique shops, restaurants, pubs, galleries and a sports store—without destroying their original charm. Gas-light style street lamps and hanging flower baskets help to maintain the neighbourhood's 19th-century atmosphere. As a result, Main Street Unionville draws everyone from film producers seeking a backdrop for period movies to thousands of tourists annually. And more are coming. The Frederick Horsman Varley Art Gallery, sitting appropriately at the end of Main Street, opened its doors to visitors in 1997. The gallery is named for one of Canada's world-famous Group of Seven painters. The late Fred Varley was one of many artists and artisans drawn to the Main Street neighbourhood. In June, the Group's creations fill Main Street when the renowned

Unionville, a distinctive community once in jeopardy of losing its historical charm in the late 1960s, now attracts many to its lovingly restored homes and businesses. Photo: Benjamin Rondel.

Unionville Festival closes the road to traffic and celebrates a community's good sense in preserving its past.

Ever since Unionville's Main Street revolt, developers know better than to ignore neighbourhood history, and none more so than those backing Markham's newer neighbourhoods in the Cornell development near the Markham Stouffville Hospital at the town's eastern edge. The hospital itself once won an award for best community service. Originally planned by the Ontario government to be a model community of 10,000 homes, Cornell was soon in the hands of private builders.

"We are in the business of building neighbourhoods, not subdivisions," says Avril Lister, vice-president of sales and marketing for the Law Development Group, one of the backers. "If you live in Cornell, you'll get to know your neighbour and you won't be further than a five-minute walk from shopping or a park."

And you won't be far from the past either. The mix of detached homes, town houses and above-the-store apartments all look as if they were designed in the 1800s and long before the automobile affronted home design. Out front, porches are prominent and there are no garage doors. Front lots are short, extending back a mere three metres from the street. On the street, the turns are restricted to ensure cars move slowly and safely through the neighbourhood. And when they do come to park, it is in garages around back of the house that are accessed by traditional laneways. Between garage and house lie narrow, but deep, backyards where people can enjoy the out-of-doors and readily communicate with neighbours as they once did over back fences.

Inside it's a different story. Cornell homes are "wired" for the future. They come equipped with a computer and digital cables which service "intelligent" appliances that know when they need repair. Older homes in Markham neighbourhoods are joining the high-tech world too, though imperceptibly from the

Milliken Mills is one of Markham's most culturally diverse communities. Here, youthful residents take time out to catch up with friends and take advantage of the recreational facilities available at the local community centre. Photo: Benjamin Rondel.

outside. Markham's enlightened zoning bylaws permit home offices and home-based businesses inside to accommodate a Markham workforce that is either "telecommuting" to jobs or self-employed. The rules also allow entrepreneurs to capitalize, albeit prudently, on Markham's history. In the tiny hamlet of Dickinson Hill, for example, a former Toronto-based communications firm is flourishing in what was once a hamlet cornerstone. The company name tells all: Gristmill Marketing.

This civic sense of what neighbourhoods need, to sustain their history and assure their future, is also reflected in Markham's seven centrally located community recreation centres. Within their walls, or usually a short jog away, they offer an arena, swimming pool, health club, squash courts, baseball diamonds, tennis courts, soccer and football fields, meeting rooms and a branch of the local library. Seasonal guides of 85 pages and more describe a myriad of year-round fitness and lifestyle-enhancing programs for all ages—from summer computer camps to ballroom dancing.

The latest Cornell development in Markham is a community that recalls the style of neighbourhoods past, yet with distinctly modern interiors that are totally wired to the future. Photo: Benjamin Rondel.

The similarities end, however, with the centres' offerings. The community centres in Thornhill, Unionville, Milliken Mills and Markham Village are as architecturally varied as their neighbourhoods.

One neighbourhood with a visible difference juts out past the end of Markham Village's Main Street, just behind the Markham Museum. That's where the Museum has preserved not only the artifacts of pioneer life but a whole 1850s neighbourhood. Visitors can get a sense of how life was then by walking into a fully restored sawmill, cider mill, slaughterhouse, village store, blacksmith's shop, Baptist church and homes fully furnished in the style of the period. The old school houses the Museum proper.

On an adjacent property, Markham Heritage Estates brings the past to life. The Estates' lots are sold by the town at below market price to buyers of heritage homes threatened by demolition. Trucked to their lots and lived in, the houses form a neighbourhood of "last resort" for Markham's residential history. It is an ingenious way to resolve the inevitable conflict felt in a burgeoning community like Markham between people determined to preserve local heritage and those pressing for new development.

The oldest of Markham's new developments are the neighbourhoods of Thornhill, a village actually shared with the neighbouring city of Vaughan. The dividing line is Yonge Street, which runs to Lake Ontario and becomes Toronto's central thoroughfare. Thornhill was first to feel the migration-enabling impact of Yonge's streetcar and later bus and subway lines as they extended northward. By the 1950s Thornhill neighbourhoods had become known as places where you could live in a village atmosphere and still conveniently work in the city.

But it is in Milliken Mills farther west along Steeles Avenue, Markham's southern road boundary, where one finds the most culturally diverse neighbourhoods. It was the first of Markham's villages to offer truly affordable housing, and many an industrious immigrant has taken rightful advantage. One benefit is a cornucopia of affordable East Indian, Caribbean, and Japanese eateries which serve a

Neighbourliness is spoken here. A strong sense of caring is present in Markham and its surrounding communities, such as Locust Hill, where this post office employee goes the extra mile with her customers— right in her own home! Photo: Benjamin Rondel.

knowledgeable and demanding clientele. Milliken Mills' multilingual populace once prompted a Markham mayor to proclaim that at least 60 languages were spoken in this town.

If one ethnic group is more in evidence than any other, it is the Chinese. A ramble through the new Pacific Mall in Milliken Mills is more like a walk through a neighbourhood mall in Hong Kong. But even as relative late-comers, Chinese developers have kept an eye on Markham's history. The Market Village shopping area that surrounds the Pacific Mall is a subtle blend of 20th-century Chinese business acumen and 19th-century-style Ontario storefronts.

Up Milliken's Kennedy Avenue and across the new electronic toll road, Highway 407, the neighbourhoods of Unionville take on a more up-market tone. Unionville residents have always shown great pride in living in an out-of-city community. Farther along the GO Train tracks that transport weary commuters home from the business wars of Toronto, Markham Village neighbourhoods display the same cared-for look as Unionville's. Modest older homes line the back streets, off Highway 48, which forms the Village's main street. Charmingly preserved and restored, they speak silently of Markham's working-class beginnings.

Wherever their village or hamlet and whatever their backgrounds, "Markhamites," as they are known, clearly look after their neighbourhoods. In 1996, they surpassed all Ontario towns in a competition for how well they cared for them; Markham won National Honours for the most effective environmental protection programs, for the most widespread community involvement, and for the best parks. Markham has also taken more than its fair share of business and industry awards. In the 1997 Ontario Marketing Awards competition, sponsored annually by the Economic Developers Council of Ontario, Markham took home four Awards of Excellence for economic development marketing: a first-place prize for its *High-Tech Business Directory*; second-place prize in the Special Event category for its *Communities in Bloom* portfolio; and a pair of third-place prizes for the "Good News" newsletter and a customer survey research report.

Markham has always been able to successfully manage its tremendous natural gifts with ambitious economic development. Over in Markham Village, Milne Park is a good example of the endurance of this legacy. The park is a 40-hectare oasis of both groomed parkland and wilderness. Its centrepiece is Milne Pond, where the reddish-brown waters of the Rouge River have been dammed into quietude. In winter it's a nice place to cross-country ski, frequently in splendid solitude, and in summer you may spot a Great Blue Heron preening itself while perched at the Pond's edge on a primordial stump. If you should observe this beautiful bird, take the time to pause and watch as it lifts to wing its way heavenwards—as if in gratitude for Markham's great bounty.

Sports enthusiasts take heart; Markham has plenty to offer! Here, local youngsters take part in a soccer match. Photo: Benjamin Rondel.

At Markham's German Mills Settlers' Park, residents have worked to maintain clean waterways as an effort in the ongoing stream rejuvenation project.
Photo: Benjamin Rondel.

26 Shaping A Destiny

During the first weekend in October, the sounds of the Markham Fair burst upon the fall air as they have every year since the 1850s.
Photos: Benjamin Rondel.

Chapter Three

Creating an Atmosphere for Business

❖ ❖ ❖

*W*hile Markham's landscape has changed dramatically from its days as a sparsely settled farming community, the area's pioneering spirit remains as fervent as ever. Currently known as Canada's high-tech capital and one of the fastest growing and most prosperous municipalities in the country, the town's exceptional locale at the northern border of Toronto is one of its primary assets. That, along with realty tax rates that are among the lowest in the Greater Toronto Area (GTA) and one of the country's highest average education levels among its residents, has made Markham an economic dynamo. The GTA is an extended urban area with more than 4 million people which includes the city of Toronto and municipalities as far east as Oshawa, as far north as Richmond Hill and as far west as Oakville.

Since 1973 Markham's population has increased by 100 per cent. It is currently estimated to be 183,000 and expected to reach 260,000 by the year 2011. Already home to more than 8,000 businesses, including a significant number of *Fortune* 500 Canadian headquarters, Markham is more than ever the scene of proliferating development for new office, manufacturing, retail and residential projects.

The town's near unprecedented growth has resulted in part due to its prime location in the heart of the GTA, named in 1996 by *Fortune* magazine as the premier metropolitan area in the world to live and work. While very much a locale with its own identity, Markham, encompassing such historic settlements as Unionville,

Photo: Benjamin Rondel

Buttonville, Milliken and Thornhill, has also harnessed its potential as part of Canada's most important metropolitan area. In fact, it has led the entire GTA in growth.

Markham's rapid transformation from a largely rural and suburban community stems from the late 1970s. At that time, fully serviced industrial land was made available at prices well below going rates in the neighbouring metropolis. The town thus counts no fewer than 16 industrial parks within its borders today, and continues to offer industrial realty taxes that are among the lowest in the region.

Not surprisingly, as industrial investment in the town increased, the role of a highly educated population, supported by the GTA's extensive network of many of the top universities and community colleges in Canada, became increasingly important. Recent Asian settlement in Markham, with Chinese the dominant language of this ever-increasing portion of the town's population, has served to extend the skill base.

"From our location in Markham, we have access to the critical skills we need to run our business," observes Robert Morine, vice-president and general manager, public sector for IBM Canada Ltd., which moved its Canadian headquarters to the municipality in the early 1980s. With over 5,000 personnel in Markham, IBM is the town's leading employer. The firm has convincingly reversed a period of corporate downsizing in its industry, and in 1997, a year featuring record domestic sales revenue, the company added more than 2,600 staff to its Canada-wide operations, a significant number of them in Markham.

IBM's initial move to the community not only paved the way for a remarkable concentration of high-tech businesses settling in Markham, but also encouraged many other major organizations in other industries to follow suit. Over 400 international and national head offices are now in Markham. That has proved mutually beneficial both to IBM and to all who followed.

Markham is home to a substantial number of Fortune *500 Canadian headquarters.*
Photo: Benjamin Rondel.

"Today we are very much a service organization, very much oriented to customer relations," says Morine, who has discovered that his company is now neighbour to many of those same customers. "What you find in Markham now is a lot of industry leaders. Actually, most industries do have a presence here."

IBM served as a magnet for other companies that located here. *Fortune* 500 companies in Markham include Ace Hardware, Johnson & Johnson, General Electric, Quaker Oats, Nike, Ford, Allstate, and Office Depot, along with such computer giants as Sun Microsystems, Digital Equipment, and Apple Canada.

Financial services represent another important cluster of economic activity in the town. Industry leader American Express is here, with well over half of its 2,300 employees across Canada based at the Markham headquarters. The firm has over 4,000 corporate clients. The American Express Foundation in Markham features such initiatives as Amex Cares Day, in support of local volunteerism, and Volunteer Action Fund, which helps groups ranging from Junior Achievement to local hospices.

Pursuing what is today a symbiotic connection with financial services, major insurance businesses have also made Markham their home. A leading example is the Allstate Insurance Company of Canada, a subsidiary of one of the largest publicly traded insurance companies in North America. Allstate constructed the 22,500-square-metre Allstate Centre in Markham in 1986. Ten years later the firm reported over $26 million in profit on nearly $400 million in premiums written, a level of activity which makes Allstate another leading employer in Markham.

Non-computer related manufacturing has also been strongly represented in the town since the 1954 arrival of Steelcase Canada, the country's largest producer of office furniture. The firm's facility occupies 64,800 square metres and has an output of 8,000 units a week. In 1957 it was followed into Markham by Emerson Electric Canada Ltd. and Cheseborough-Ponds (Canada) Inc. These three pioneering firms were followed by Canac Kitchens, LEGO, Pillsbury, Polygram, Timex, Pioneer and Toshiba, to name a few.

Industries both large and small find an excellent advocate in the Markham Board of Trade. Robert Kiefer, Chairman of the more than 850-member Board of Trade from June 1997 to June 1998, emphasizes that membership includes everything from the self-employed individual to those organizations on the scale of IBM. "Markham is the hub of York Region," Kiefer says with pride. "It has certainly been positioned as the high-tech capital of Canada, but there is much more to Markham than just high technology. There is a lot of residential development happening, which, in turn, brings new businesses and developers."

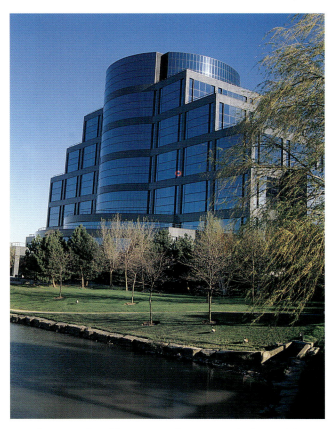

The town of Markham's prime location, at the heart of the Greater Toronto Area, is just one of the reasons so many leading businesses have chosen to locate here. Photo: Benjamin Rondel.

The Board of Trade's three-year strategic plan has had very specific objectives. In 1995-96, the idea was to build core competency within the organization along with an emphasis on networking and facilitating business. In 1996-97, the goal was to "create member value." For the 1997-99 time frame, the accent is on growing the member base and raising the profile of the Board in the community. Joint memberships, provided through a partnership agreement with the Scarborough-York Region Chinese Business Association, provide an avenue for the Board to accomplish both these objectives.

Increasingly, Markham looks to the future with a world vision. For example, the town has an active International Economic Alliance program, linking Markham's business community to business centres in the USA, Hong Kong, Israel and Jordan.

In a town geared to cutting-edge industries, Markham has, not surprisingly, taken a striking contemporary approach to some of its recent residential-commercial developments. Near the Markham-Stouffville Hospital at the eastern edge of the municipality, for instance, new housing projects have been designed with a sharp departure from standard subdivision creation.

Taking what is sometimes called a "neo-urbanism" approach, the latest communities near the hospital emphasize scales and settings closer to those of an historic Ontario village than a typically sprawling suburb dominated by cars. In these communities, a community square is within five minutes of the farthest house in each development module. The square features shops, basic services and office space for those who want to work within walking distance of home.

For those who work from their residence, Markham has been one of the first municipalities to actively encourage the home-office trend. The town is known for its flexibility in the matter of establishing a business in a residence, an undertaking often subject to numerous outdated restrictions elsewhere.

Naturally, proximity to retail amenities and other services provides a bonus for Markham residents, but the current spate of growth is creating an even more impressive series of new developments. The Galleria, a 53-hectare land parcel located at Highways 7 and 407, is transforming into 180,000 square metres of retail, office and recreation space, in addition to town house and

Markham's realty tax rates, among the lowest in the GTA, have contributed to the town's unprecedented growth. Photo: Benjamin Rondel.

Shaping a Destiny 31

high-rise developments. The Galleria is the largest recent example of a major residential/commercial project in keeping with Markham's vision for large-scale mixed development.

Other examples of growth abound. New shopping centres include Pacific Mall (24,750 square metres), Commerce Gate (14,895 square metres), First Markham Place (13,500 square metres) and Cachet Centre (13,050 square metres).

Markham's excellent physical accessibility has long been one of the town's chief assets. More than half of North America's industrial market, with over 130 million customers, is within a single day's trucking distance of Markham, which is served by several of Ontario's largest highways.

The latest in this network of state-of-the-art highways is the 407 ETR, an express toll route that employs state-of-the-art electronic toll collection technology. Without waiting in long lines at payment booths, as is required on traditional toll roads, regular commuters simply have a small electronic device attached to the rear-view mirrors of their vehicles. Overhead electronic sensors on the route mark the vehicle's entrance and exit points, with a monthly billing system in place rather than daily roadside transactions involving cash, tickets or tokens.

A 69-kilometre east-west road, the 407 ETR runs parallel to one of the busiest thoroughfares in North America, Highway 401, which extends to the Windsor-Detroit border crossing in the west and virtually all the way to Montreal in the east. Of course, the 401 also connects numerous points in the Greater Toronto Area. The addition of the 407 gives Markham an important central artery that brings needed convenience to the greatly expanded community. Significant, too, is that the new toll highway will be self-sustaining and will impose no tax burden on the municipality.

Meanwhile, Markham's Toronto Buttonville Municipal Airport acts as an executive-class airport, and in its own right is the 10th busiest airport in the country, with over 200,000 take-offs and landings each year. The Flight Training

Above: What sets Markham apart from other municipalities is its common-sense approach to balancing quality-of-life issues with ongoing development and economic prosperity. Photo: Benjamin Rondel.

Right: Markham's many leading technology firms have given the town its well-deserved reputation of being Canada's high-tech capital. Photo: Benjamin Rondel.

Markham's Toronto Buttonville Municipal Airport is the 10th busiest airport in Canada, with more than 200,000 take-offs and landings each year.
Photo: Benjamin Rondel.

School at Buttonville has an international reputation and attracts student pilots from all over the world. Toronto's Pearson International Airport is only a 30-minute drive from Markham.

Rail freight access via Canada's two national railways, Canadian Pacific and Canadian National, links Markham to a network of 33,000 kilometres of track through a series of cross-border gateways to the United States. GO Train passenger service rapidly connects Markham commuters to the financial district of downtown Toronto, although the municipality's concentration of corporate operations has, over time, actually decreased the need to conduct business downtown.

Today, of course, much of the movement in and out of Markham is no longer by road, sky or track; it is electronic. The town has launched TeleMarkham, a rapidly expanding telecommunications infrastructure that has made the municipality a leading corporate call centre location in Canada with major banks, insurance firms and high-tech organizations creating national call centres for customer service.

In this regard, Markham shares and leads a GTA competitive advantage in telecommunications: the GTA is North America's only major metropolitan area serviced entirely by digital public network switching. The GTA also features one of North America's most heavily ringed fibre-

The 407 ETR is an express toll route that features state-of-the-art electronic toll collection technology.
Photo: Benjamin Rondel.

34 Shaping A Destiny

optics systems, as well as the longest cellular corridor in the world.

Markham isn't only about development, of course. The town also features 680 hectares of parks and nature preserves in addition to manicured tracts of green that comprise 14 golf courses, including Angus Glen, which was named Canada's best new course in 1996. (Markham is a natural for golfers since 26 courses are within a 30-minute drive.) As it happens, such a local emphasis on green dovetails with Markham's appeal to the environmental protection sector. About 70 per cent of this particular Canadian industry is in Ontario, with many prominent firms located in Markham, which, by the way, has been a leader in municipal waste management since 1970, when Ontario's first municipally operated recycling depot opened within its borders.

In 1992, Markham received the Recycling Council of Ontario's "Ontario Waste Minimization Award" for tangible waste reduction and diversion, as well as innovative public education programs. Markham also launched a long-term waste management strategy with its "Model Community Demonstration Project"; it initially involved over 5,000 households. Throughout the 1990s, Markham expanded its paper fibre collection program and, in 1996, received the Recycling Council of Ontario's "Gold Medal for Waste Reduction."

Green space and recreational amenities are not mere by-products of a prosperous community like Markham; rather, quality-of-life concerns have always been an integral aspect of the community's economic success. Five recreation centres, a first-rate theatre and arts program, an historical museum and the newly completed Fredrick Horsman Varley Art Gallery are examples of how Markham's investment in lifestyle amenities have been part and parcel of its business growth.

And growth, in turn, has meant looking farther afield for opportunity. An irony in Markham's designation as a town is that the community is hardly a self-contained "burb" focused just on local concerns. In pursuit of new business relations, the municipality signed an agreement in 1996 with the community of Laval in the province of Quebec. The move was not a mere public relations gesture, but a first step in economic cooperation that will bring competitive advantages to both parties. Laval, which sits in roughly the same relation to Montreal as Markham does to Toronto, also shares a number of Markham's key economic development attractions.

What sets Markham apart from many other municipalities, however, is its common-sense approach to balancing quality-of-life issues with ongoing development and economic prosperity. Markham has not only managed to preserve the very fabric and texture of its waterways and parklands, but has ensured that the local citizenry will continue to cherish and protect these amenities.

GO Train passenger service rapidly connects Markham commuters to downtown Toronto.
Photo: Benjamin Rondel.

Shaping a Destiny 35

Chapter Four

Establishing High-Tech Connections
❖ ❖ ❖

*T*he new world of fibre optics and increasingly sophisticated computer technology came face-to-face with the old in 1982 when a sprawling, 10-hectare expanse of land in Markham opened its doors as the new Canadian headquarters of IBM. It was just beyond Steeles and Victoria Park Avenues, at the northeast corner of this intersection, where the new Markham began. IBM Canada had moved its head office from several miles to the south in Toronto. Few people realized it at the time, but "Silicon Valley North" had just come into being.

IBM's building—a massive complex of glass and steel encompassing almost 81,000 square metres on a campus-like setting—still stands as one of Markham's most recognizable and visible landmarks. In fact, it's impossible to miss the impressive structure which continues to retain a futuristic aura about it. What is even more important is that it was IBM's decision to locate in Markham that blazed a trail for other high-tech companies to follow.

Indeed, like plants taking root after a torrential downpour, high-tech players—everyone from small, innovative software start-ups to huge, multinational hardware manufacturers—began locating in Markham after IBM broke the ice, and the once sedate town was then forever transformed. The thinking at the time was that if a company with the stature and savvy of IBM saw a promising future in this tranquil community, who could argue?

Photo: First Light

Then, along came another big player in the high-tech industry—namely, Apple Canada Incorporated. The floodgates were now open.

The early arrivals were followed by Johnson Controls Limited, which manufactures sensors; Ford Electronics Manufacturing Corporation, with its worldwide mandate to manufacture electronic components for Ford automobiles; Mitsubishi Electric Sales Canada Incorporated, which made electronic business products; and ATI Technologies Incorporated, which manufactures graphics accelerator boards and personal computer components. And there were others. Many of them. It didn't matter if it was portables or printers, LANs or WANs, mainframes or modems; if the technology had anything to do with Canada's burgeoning super information highway, then it was very likely that this technology was being manufactured, distributed and/or warehoused right here in Markham.

Stephen Chait, Markham's Director of Economic Development, recalls the day when IBM opened shop. He says that while Markham was beneficial for IBM, the company was also beneficial for Markham. "IBM instantly created an address for us," he says. "From 1982 onward, the word 'Markham' was suddenly becoming very familiar in corporate offices throughout the entire world."

This indirect advertising only served to attract yet more interest in the town. Throughout the 1980s, when the high-tech sector really began to proliferate in Markham, the construction of distribution centres, office towers and industrial parks flourished in the community. An oft-repeated wisecrack at the time was that the official bird of Markham was the crane—the construction crane—since so many of them were peppering the town's landscape.

Over the years, the high-tech migration to Markham has continued. More recent arrivals have included such companies as Synervoice (a developer of computerized voice processing applications), 3D Microcomputers (a manufacturer and distributor of microcomputer systems and components), CyberTrends Inc. (an Internet provider and designer of Web sites), Stirling Douglas Group (a software

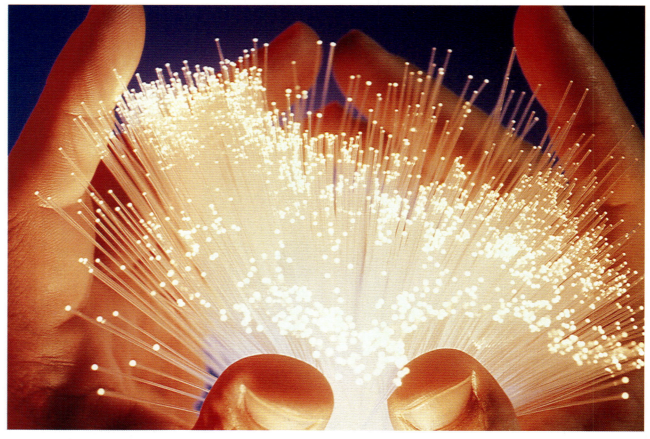

Integrated into a national network, Markham's fibre-optic access lines move information across Canada and around the world, providing the town with a leading-edge communications infrastructure. Photo: First Light.

development firm for the retail industry), and Digital Processing Systems (a computer hardware manufacturer). And the pulse has gone on and on.

Markham soon became home to more than 600 high-tech companies with a staggering 25 per cent of all its jobs in the high-tech sector. The industry has played a huge part in the dramatic growth of Markham and the metamorphosis of the town into Canada's Silicon Valley North. Just look at the population. Back in 1971, Markham's population was only 31,000. By 1989 it had surpassed 135,000, and in 1991 it was 159,000. In the year 2011, the total population of Markham is expected to exceed one quarter of a million people. This means that the number of the town's inhabitants will have grown by a phenomenal 800 per cent in 40 years, or an average of 20 per cent a year over four decades!

So what is it about Markham that attracted and continues to attract the likes of IBM, Apple, Digital and an abundance of other high-tech companies both large and small? In fact, there are several tangible benefits to locating in the town. First, there is the location aspect of Markham and its easy proximity to downtown Toronto, but without the congestion. This is a key attribute. Also, being at the cross-section of major super highways (401, 407 and 400) doesn't hurt either. Thus, Markham is ideally positioned in terms of access.

And for those who prefer taking to the skies, Markham can serve up an airport. Toronto Buttonville Municipal Airport, which is located right in the heart of Markham, is popular with many local business executives. It makes for a congestion-free alternative to Lester B. Pearson International Airport in Mississauga or downtown Toronto's Island Airport.

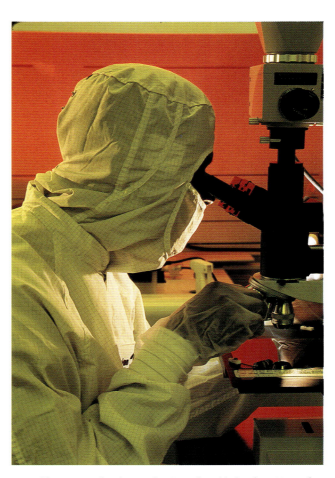

Markham's membership in the Canadian Technology Network, an initiative of Canada's National Research Council, means the town has access to solutions to technology-based problems and more. Photo: First Light.

Probably the biggest advantage of Markham, of course, is low property taxes, which, in some cases, is half of the rate levied by neighbouring municipalities. This is undoubtedly a most significant lure. What's more, although Markham has undergone rapid development since the arrival of Big Blue in 1982, there is still a ready supply of fully serviced and vacant industrial land available in choice locations. Indeed, the town's 16 main industrial areas and business parks permit a wide range of industrial and commercial use. They range in price from $250,000 to $600,000 per acre with industrial lease rates ranging from $3 to $7.50 per square foot.

Another selling point that has attracted high-tech players is Markham's first-rate communications infrastructure. Markham has fibre-optic access lines integrated into a national fibre-optic network that moves information across the country and around the globe. The town's communications infrastructure matches or exceeds that available in major cities in the U.S. and around the world.

On top of all this, the town's administration has been hailed for embracing a "can-do" attitude when it comes to helping business. For example, Markham maintains active alliances with municipalities in the U.S., the U.K., Israel and the Far East. In addition, the economic development office provides contacts for business people and can identify opportunities specific to the high-tech area. A good example of this is its role in assisting small companies in the licensing of their software in foreign countries.

Markham is also a member of the Canadian Technology Network, an initiative of Canada's National Research Council. This helps the town source solutions to technology-based problems and means that Markham can do such things as help a company with a new kind of manufacturing system, provide advice for a technology provider, or even enhance a new network opportunity.

As long as Markham has been a home, and a magnet, for the high-tech industry, the local government has been very pro-business and very anti-red

A Markham resident since 1969, Mayor Don Cousens has witnessed the town's population increase from 35,000 to 183,000 people. Photo: Alan Marsh.

tape. In short, it's the kind of municipal environment that the private sector loves.

The town provides a multitude of services for high-tech companies who may be considering Markham as a home base. For example, there is a database with information on available office and industrial space, land, builders and even realtors who can assist companies in site selection. For those companies interested in exporting, Markham's economic development office can link companies to the proper planner, agency or country. The office also hosts incoming and outgoing visits to bring together companies who might be looking for customers. If that's not enough, for those entrepreneurs just starting out, Markham's Small Business Self-Help Office offers a wealth of advice and information, and get this—all this advice and information is absolutely free!

It's clear Markham has traditionally had a local government that is sympathetic and supportive of a company's needs, and it should. Mayor Don Cousens is from the high-tech sector himself.

"I have lived here since 1969 and seen the population go from 35,000 people to 183,000," says Cousens, who has been the mayor since 1994. Prior to that, he was an elected member of the Ontario Legislature, and he also spent many years with Honeywell Bull Limited. "Markham has become a very, very strong business community over the years. I think it began to evolve into a high-tech sector when IBM established its headquarters here. That made us a magnet for other high-tech companies, and now, of course, we have over 650 high-tech companies in town."

Cousens is quick to mention that Markham has one of the lowest tax rates in the Greater Toronto Area. In addition to that, it can boast of one attribute which is virtually unheard of in the downtown Toronto corridor. What's that? Free parking. Lots of it. In the popular board game of *Monopoly*, "Free Parking" denotes winning the jackpot, and that's pretty well what it's like in Markham. Yes, if there is one element of modernization that is hard to find in this town, it's that urban scourge known as the parking meter.

It shouldn't be surprising that Markham is the home of the York Technology Association, a networking forum which takes action on issues important to stakeholders in the technology community. The association's formation coincided with IBM's arrival in 1982 and was co-founded by Cousens himself. In its inaugural year, the York Technology Association received a $100,000 start-up grant from the town.

The association eventually became self-sustaining, and it wasn't long before it was the largest high-tech organization in all of Canada. The group's 120 member companies interact with all levels of government, as well as with other national trade associations. Markham, of course, is a logical fit for such an organization, since 75 per cent of Canada's computer software and hardware revenues are generated from within a 32-kilometre radius of the town.

"What we've got in Markham is a business community that not only has the high-technology companies, but an entrepreneurial spirit," says Mark McAlister, executive director of the York Technology Association. "In other words, the people locating in Markham are entrepreneurs with business savvy. They want to be close to others who have a track record of success in the global market."

Indeed, McAlister says the ability of YTA members to make solid connections is another key in choosing Markham as a Canadian headquarters site. "If somebody decides to build their high-tech business here, the reason they are doing so is because they don't need to go to California's Silicon Valley to make strategic partnerships. They can probably find that strategic partner in their own industrial park or even their own building, for that matter.

"But, in fact, I really don't think we necessarily are Silicon Valley North. We are really a different kettle of fish. We're more like a mix of Silicon Valley and Wall Street. We have a combination of technical ability, entrepreneurial firepower, and access to capital, banking and professional services. Markham is a business community that is unequalled in Canada."

IBM Canada's Mike Quinn adds that Markham seemed to hit all the right buttons when the company made the move. Manager of corporate public relations for IBM Canada, Quinn recalled the reasons why the town was so appealing a place for the company's new headquarters.

"Markham offered competitive tax rates," he says. "We already had a significant employee base in northeast Toronto, which isn't far from Markham, and the site we chose gave us excellent access to major highway routes as well as to public transit in both Toronto and Markham."

Quinn goes on to say that the company also wanted to have a campus-like setting, and this was very possible in Markham. In fact, he says many people compare IBM Canada's HQR site, which employs more than 4,000 people, to that of a university campus. The site is much more than a traditional headquarters, since it also serves as an education and training facility. One might even say that it's user-friendly. Just like Markham.

Indeed, Markham proved so conducive to doing business that by 1985—three short years after IBM arrived—that same company was already in expansion mode. It built a state-of-the-art distribution facility, a building with 38,700 square metres, not to mention an additional 400 people.

So what does the future hold for Silicon Valley North? If the more recent arrivals are any indication, yet more high-tech companies are going to be Markham-bound. The growth has continued unabatedly. From one year to the next, thousands of square metres of industrial space have been occupied by companies attracted to Markham, bringing literally thousands of jobs to the local community.

The area's many golf courses provide hours of recreational enjoyment for Markham business executives and entrepreneurs. Photo: Benjamin Rondel.

None of this surprises Mark McAlister of the York Technology Association. He succinctly sums up the business community's love affair with the town. "A very big part of Markham's success is that, for the most part, the people who work on staff at the town have a good orientation to business. The whole idea is understanding what business needs and then realizing when to help, and when to get out of the way."

The IBM building stands as one of Markham's most recognizable landmarks. The company blazed a trail in Markham for the relocation of many other high-tech companies. Photo: Benjamin Rondel.

Chapter Five

Turning Progress into Prosperity

❖ ❖ ❖

Markham's Chinese Community

*I*n the 200 years since the days when Markham's claim to fame was its prime farmland, a surprising evolution has occured, distinguishing the city as one of the most prosperous in Canada, if not all of North America. And while that may sound like rapid development, a far more astonishing change has been taking place in one of Markham's ethnic groups—its Chinese community.

Ivy Lee is an excellent example of this changing perspective in Markham. She isn't an imposing woman when you meet her. She does, however, walk with a hurried pace—which doesn't surprise you when you learn that she works 14 hours a day. She is what you call an entrepreneur. Ivy is the publisher of *Modesty* magazine, which, at its inception in 1994, was one of the few independent Chinese magazines around. Boasting 10,000 readers, it carries articles about food, entertainment, politics, money and finance. Her editor says it's particularly heavy in the latter category, which is understandable when you consider that its readers are generally well-to-do, a trait shared by many among Markham's Chinese community.

Ivy is not just a magazine publisher, however. She also publishes books and corporate annual reports, and if that's not enough, she runs two other businesses as well. One is a training centre for young artists, and the other is a massage clinic.

Photo: Benjamin Rondel

Ivy immigrated to Canada in 1979 from her native Singapore, where she was a garment factory proprietor and ran a dressmaking school. After coming to Canada, she first worked as a waitress and a keypunch operator, but then studied massage therapy and eventually went into business for herself. You might say she's a member of the Chinese Canadian "who's who"—in fact, there is a page in an annual Chinese directory devoted exclusively to her.

"Before coming here I applied to five countries," she says: "Canada, Australia, the United Kingdom, the United States and Taiwan. Canada was the first to respond. I think I made a good decision with Canada, though. There is no discrimination. They promote multiculturalism. I think this is the best country in the world."

Ivy is just one of the many hardworking Chinese entrepreneurs now residing in Markham. And if Markham is one of Canada's most affluent communities, then its Chinese population must surely be one of its most affluent ethnic groups. It's also the largest, comprising well over one-third of all inhabitants. Just drive along the winding arteries which snake through the modern new subdivisions resplendent with spacious, two-storey homes and you get the idea. And when you drive past the shopping centers decorated with Chinese signage, you begin to realize this is Asian country.

For all intents, the Pacific Mall and adjacent Market Square, located on a large tract of land at the intersection of Steeles and Kennedy Avenues in Markham, constitute the new home of the Greater Toronto Area's Chinese community. This is the largest Asian shopping centre in North America with over 300 stores in Pacific Mall and about another 200 in Market Square. Once inside the mall, you feel as if you've been transported to Southeast Asia, since most of the goods available for purchase are imported from Hong Kong, Singapore, Malaysia or Thailand. For the most part, the shops are small businesses offering clothing, arts and crafts, foods, shoes and cosmetics. There are also many specialty shops like the herbal consultant or Shark's Fin City, which sells this popular and elegant Chinese food; indeed, a pair of one-metre shark fins are prominently on display behind a mounted glass.

Literally everything in and around this focal point of Markham's Chinese community has been built since 1990. What were once bucolic orchards of apple and peach trees have been transformed into a bustling, urban extravaganza of retail shopping, entertainment, and the proverbial "good life." Pacific Mall opened in December, 1996, and on the inside it's almost like a trade show, the individual proprietors marketing their wares within the neat confines of their respective shops, each of them separated by glass partitions. Built almost exclusively by Hong Kong investors, Pacific Mall does include some rather high-profile players as well, such as the Bank of East Asia (Canada).

Most days, the traffic around this area is pretty congested. As Ivy says, while impatiently waiting in a lineup of vehicles at a stoplight, "I can tell the economy is getting better by all the traffic. The best time to drive in Markham is between 10 a.m. and 3 p.m."

Markham deservedly has the reputation of a young, thriving community with a local government that is appealing to business. There is plenty of land available, and relatively low taxes. Put all these things together and it's easy to see why so many affluent Hong Kong Chinese have chosen to come here over other centres.

To say that Kit Wong, first president of the Richmond Hill-Markham Chinese Business Association, is "plugged in" to the Chinese community would be a gross understatement. He runs an automobile leasing company, and his office is full of plaques and citations from such organizations as the Toronto Cathay Lion's Club, Chinese Bowling Congress, Toronto Chinese Golf Association, York Central

Ivy Lee, Markham publisher and entrepreneur, chose the business-friendly atmosphere of Markham.
Photo: Alan Marsh.

44 Shaping A Destiny

Hospital, of which he is a trustee, as well as his business association. Not surprisingly, he has been approached by several political parties to run as a candidate.

Wong talks about the history of Chinese immigration to the Greater Toronto Area and puts the present reality of Markham into perspective. It started with the original Chinatown which first took root in downtown Toronto. There were a few grocery stores and Chinese restaurants, and, in fact, the city's very first Chinese Business Association started strictly as a restaurant association. The community was largely comprised of lower income, and poorly educated, residents. The community grew and started to spread out, its centre in the Dundas Street-Spadina Avenue area. Later, another large Chinese community began to flourish in the eastern suburbs of Scarborough before advancing northward.

Unquestionably, Hong Kong's impending return to mainland China in 1997 was the catalyst that brought many of the younger, and more affluent, Chinese to the Toronto region, and ultimately to Markham. "It started around 1992," says Wong, "and Markham was the place to go. It wasn't Vancouver because there were no job opportunities for young people there. It wasn't Ottawa or Montreal. It was here. You have the big city next door, and in Markham you have good schools, good transportation, a clean environment and low crime. You have land, big homes and low taxes. This was the place to be."

Other focal points of the community soon developed, along with the schools, subdivisions and shopping malls. The Cham Shan Temple at Bayview and Steeles, initially built in 1973, had to be expanded to serve an ever-growing congregation 20 years later. Not long after that, the Markham Chinese Baptist Church was built on Valleywood Drive. And while these temples and other places of worship were important pillars of the Chinese community, the most important pillar of all was, and is, business.

Kit Wong, president of the Richmond Hill-Markham Chinese Business Association, credits Markham's transportation, good schools, clean environment and low crime for the growing Chinese population.
Photo: Alan Marsh.

When the real influx of Chinese immigrants occurred in the early 1990s, there was an obvious need for a local, specifically Chinese business association. What began as a casual business luncheon attended by a banker, a golf equipment retailer and a restaurateur quickly evolved into a steering committee with 15 business persons of influence in the community. In 1993, the association was officially registered with the Government of Ontario. Its mission? To assist members in all aspects of doing business in the region, and to help mainstream businesses tap into the lucrative Asian markets domestically and internationally.

Wong admits that the Chinese community isolated itself from mainstream Canada because of linguistic and cultural barriers. But the association, he says, has tried to stimulate more Chinese participation in the local community while, at the same time, preserving the Chinese culture and heritage.

While the new Chinese-owned shopping malls cater to the local Chinese community, the performances held at Market Village every Sunday afternoon are multicultural. One Sunday may see a performance of Edelweiss dancers from Germany followed the next week by a showcase of Greek songs and dances, or a dance company from the Ukraine.

In January 1998, the local Chinese business community took a big step forward with the formation of the Confederation of Greater Toronto Chinese Business Associations. There have been four such associations in the area, but the new umbrella organization brings them together with a much more powerful voice— about 2,300 members in all. Yolanda Chan is serving her third term as president of the Scarborough-York Region Chinese Business Association, which represents

The Cham Shan Temple, at Bayview and Steeles Avenues in Markham, has served an ever-growing congregation since 1973. Photo: Alan Marsh.

more than 300 businesses, many of them in Markham. She says the new association may just be the largest ethnic business organization in Canada.

"We want to have a united voice," says Yolanda, who is a financial advisor, manager and a significant asset portfolio administrator. She is also founder of Goldense International, a business-to-business consulting firm specializing in China-Canada business opportunities. "Our own association has been very active in bridging cultural, health, business and financial issues. In the last five years, especially, the local Asian community has grown substantially, and a lot of these immigrants need assistance with city hall or setting up a business. Among other things, we serve as a liaison to various levels of government."

Last November, Yolanda and the presidents of the other three Chinese business associations spent three weeks in China along with Chinese business leaders from the United States, Australia and New Zealand. The idea was to help build a bridge for Chinese businesspeople in these countries. The president of the Republic of China himself gave them a reception.

Although the Chinese factor in Markham is relatively new, the Chinese are anything but new to Canada. In 1885, the Canadian Pacific Railway was completed in western Canada largely by Chinese workers. The Chinese in Canada at the time were either laying tracks for the railway or employed as laundry workers; about 90 per cent of these early Chinese immigrants were labourers earning from $10 to $25 a month. In those days, the Canadian government levied a head tax of $50 per Chinese person upon entry, and by 1903 that tax had jumped to $500, which was quite a tidy sum for the day. Discrimination against Chinese was common, and two anti-Chinese riots actually broke out in Vancouver, in 1887 and 1907. It wasn't until the Second World War, when Canada became an ally to China with its declaration of war against Japan, that relations improved. By war's end, the Chinese had succeeded in gaining citizens' rights in Canada, and in 1947 the Chinese Community Centre of Ontario was established.

Pacific Mall is the largest Asian shopping centre in North America. Photo: Alan Marsh.

In 1982, the first wave of immigrants from Hong Kong began arriving in Toronto and Vancouver, what with increasing concern over that colony's future under a Chinese government. Then, in 1984, the signing of the Joint Declaration between the United Kingdom and China resulted in a huge flow of funds and technical staff from Hong Kong to North America. Just five years later, more than 30,000 Chinese staged a massive rally in Toronto to support the pro-democracy movement in Beijing, and the ensuing massacre at Tiananmen Square no doubt convinced more than one Hong Kong family that the time to leave had arrived. By 1992, Markham had become the destination of choice.

So affluent were these new Hong Kong Chinese immigrants that it was estimated each one brought $250,000 or more to the country. A book entitled *Hong Kong Money* reported that Hong Kong investors had contributed a staggering $8 trillion to Canada's manufacturing and real estate industries during the boom years of the early to mid-1990s.

It didn't take long for three Chinese newspapers to emerge in the Greater Toronto Area: the *Sing Tao* newspaper, the Taiwan-funded *World Journal,* and the *Sing Pao Daily News*. Tony Wan, who is the editor of Ivy Lee's *Modesty* magazine, has worked at both the *World Journal* and *Sing Pao Daily News*. A very youthful-looking 50, he says that most of the Hong Kong Chinese who lived in the eastern suburbs of Toronto were of lower income, but that in the late 1980s this had all started to change.

"People feared Communism," he says. "The Chinese eventually moved from downtown Toronto to Scarborough and then to Markham. But, starting in the late 1980s, the only people who came were wealthy people."

This wealth and prosperity brought investment in the arts and culture. The Chinese Cultural Centre of Greater Toronto is a non-profit, non-political organization located just south of Markham in the Toronto suburb of Scarborough. Boasting an art gallery, a fully computerized resource centre, and a state-of-the-art theatre, it is the largest Chinese Cultural Centre in North America. Construction began in late 1996 and, when completed, the Cultural Centre will be a magnet for all of the Chinese in the Greater Toronto Area. Though it is not actually in Markham, it is conveniently located just a short drive from Pacific Mall and Market Square.

Providing a united voice for member businesses, the Scarborough-York Region Chinese Business Association represents more than 300 companies. Photo: Alan Marsh.

The fall of 1996 was also notable for two other important launches in Markham's Chinese community. The New China Bookstore (Canada) Ltd. opened its doors in the Fortino Mall at Kennedy and Denison in October of that year. The largest Chinese bookstore in Canada, it distributes and retails books, audio and videotapes, newspapers, magazines, compact discs and stationery. One month later, the Markham *Communicator*, a newspaper that publishes in both English and Chinese, published its first issue. Publisher Julie Wang-Morris said her objective was to help the people of Markham bridge cultural and racial gaps.

"It is human nature to stereotype a group of people, whether racially, socially or economically," she said. "But those who ignore groups on the grounds of race or culture deny a social reality. The multilingual market is becoming more and more a force to be reckoned with. They're coming here with cash and are ready to spend like you wouldn't believe."

Yes, the Chinese community of modern Markham is indeed a far cry from those early immigrants who toiled for meager wages on the Canadian Pacific Railway. Today, Chinese residents are investment bankers, executives running high-tech companies, financial advisors, publishers and professionals, such as doctors, dentists and accountants. They are also businesspeople and entrepreneurs like Ivy Lee. Fortunately for Markham, some of them are still in the food business, and the town lays claim to many of the best-quality restaurants serving Chinese cuisine in the GTA, offering everything from the grandiose establishment with stunning decor to the simple takeout service. Choices include Cantonese, Hong Kong-style western food, vegetarian and noodle specialties, as well as Peking and northern Chinese cuisine. A large number of the restaurants congregate along Woodbine Avenue and Kennedy Road and, make no mistake, there are many of them. What's more, they're all listed on their very own Web sites! Without a doubt, the Chinese have come a long way since the first wave of immigrants arrived in Canada. Especially those in Markham.

Chapter Six

Shaping the Spirit of Markham
❖ ❖ ❖
Arts & Culture

*T*he people of Markham would never dream of merely building a community—highly advanced in business and technology—without also giving rightful place to culture and the arts. Today, Markham boasts a vibrant arts scene, and facilities to match, that are much more ambitious than a municipality this size might seem to warrant at first glance. Then again, these cultural roots run deep.

Frederick Horsman Varley lived and worked out of a studio in the community of Unionville for the last 12 years of his life. The studio was in a Gothic Revival-style cottage at 197 Main Street in the historic section of town. Varley, a gifted portrait artist and a founding member of Canada's famous Group of Seven, was effectively sponsored during this time by local resident Kathleen Gormley McKay and her husband, Donald. The house had been built by Kathleen's great-grandfather, Salem Eckhardt, in the 1840s.

Varley died in 1969, leaving Kathleen a rich legacy of his paintings and the works of his contemporaries. Nine years later she sold her historic house to the town of Markham, and today it stands as the Kathleen Gormley McKay Art Centre, a venue for exhibitions by local artists and art classes. And what of her valuable collection of 80 oil paintings? Why, she bequeathed it to the town, of course.

Indeed, the Frederick Horsman Varley Art Gallery of Markham was opened in May, 1997, at the corner of Main Street and Carlton Road.

Photo: Benjamin Rondel

This environmentally controlled facility is the only art gallery in Canada that is devoted to a single member of the Group of Seven. Ironically, the opening took place only a few short months after Kathleen passed away at the age of 97.

In the traditional grass-roots style of Markham, the community played a major part in fund-raising, while the federal and provincial governments each chipped in a third of the cost; the remaining third was raised locally. And so the spirit of one of Canada's greatest artists, whose canvases brought out the best of the pioneer spirit, continues, and the community is that much richer for it. In addition to the permanent collection, the Gallery hosts exhibitions from local, national and international sources, and features group tours, school programs, studio courses, lectures and workshops for local artists.

Having an art gallery of such stature is obviously a coup for Markham, but it's certainly not the only cultural achievement of this vibrant community that clearly values and embodies the philosophy of making a place where people want to work as well as live.

The Markham Theatre for Performing Arts, located at the northwest corner of Warden Avenue and Highway 7, was opened in 1985 to much acclaim. In its first decade of existence, this impressive facility did better than just answer the bell as a focal point of the arts in Markham, as more than 1 million people passed through its doors.

The elegant theatre includes a 528-seat auditorium with absolutely first-rate acoustics, and smaller rooms which are dubbed the Rehearsal Hall and the Artists' Lounge. Both these rooms are equipped with skylights, which are a nice touch for intimate meetings serving groups of 15 to 150 people.

The Markham Theatre for Performing Arts very much embodies the theme of "community." As well as being a showplace for top professional entertainment, it serves as an artistic training ground for new young local talent, and is home to several community arts

Named for one of Canada's greatest artists, the Frederick Horsman Varley Art Gallery in Markham hosts exhibitions from local, national and international sources, and features group tours, school programs, studio courses, lectures and workshops for local artists.
Photo: Alan Marsh.

Not all learning takes place in the classroom! This young artist focuses on the details of a still life in a children's art class at the Frederick Horsman Varley Art Gallery.
Photo: Alan Marsh.

groups. Some of the most well-known names from the Markham business community are actively involved as sponsors, and the list includes the likes of such companies as Allstate, Bell, Consumers Gas, IBM, NCR, Royal Bank and TD Bank. As far as productions are concerned, in its relatively brief history the theatre has played host to such world-renowned performers as Cleo Laine, as well as Canada's own top musical talent, including internationally acclaimed contralto Maureen Forrester, rock and roll legend Rompin' Ronnie Hawkins and The Nylons. The theatre attracts dance and dramatic productions as well, everything from *The Nutcracker* to *Dracula*.

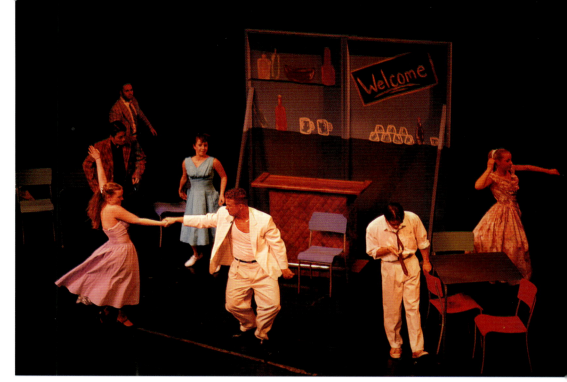

Performance offerings of Markham's Theatre for Performing Arts include classical music, dance and live theatre. Photo: Alan Marsh.

This blend of professional and local community involvement says much about Markham. No fewer than six local artistic groups perform regularly at the theatre. Musically speaking, the 60-member Markham Concert Band performs a series of five concerts a year at the theatre, while the even larger York Symphony Orchestra performs four. And then there's the Markham Men of Harmony, a collection of barbershop quartets with more than 70 members in total, which also performs regularly.

In terms of the dramatic arts, the Markham Little Theatre, which had its roots in the 1960s, does four plays a year. The Unionville Theatre Company, which encourages young people to get involved in live theatre, performs one major show a year. And then there is the Markham Youth Theatre, set up and run by high school and college students, which performs one or two events annually.

In fact, the theatre's strong ties to young people are as strong as brick and mortar. When the Markham Theatre for Performing Arts was established in 1985, it was physically connected to another new building, Unionville High School. The school's Arts York program, which offers credit courses in drama, music, dance and the visual arts, attracts students from all over York Region, who can use the theatre as a great learning tool.

"This is very much a community theatre," says David Scott, who is involved in the theatre management. "We have a strong educational component with not only the high school, but also with separate schools and elementary schools. When the theatre was built, a decision was made that arts would be a focus of the community, and it says something about the people of Markham. They want to see classical music, good dance performances and live theatre."

Every year, a number of students from throughout York Region focus on Unionville High School to further their interests in dance, music, drama, and visual arts, and their access to the theatre is obviously a tremendous boon to them. The three-year, co-operative education program at the high school also provides students with practical experience in some "behind-the-scenes" skills such as lighting, audio, and staging. The program has been very successful; many students have gone on to post-secondary studies and even professional careers in these disciplines.

While the theatre and art gallery are relative newcomers to the landscape of Markham, one can't forget that the history of this community goes back to the pioneer days, and those days have been preserved at the Markham Museum and Heritage Village. It calls itself a "community museum" and it is. Markham was once the centre for carriage manufacturing in Ontario, and the museum features an impressive exhibit devoted to this important era. Another exhibit called the

"Urban Frontier" is interactive; it takes visitors from the first native settlements right to the vibrant Markham of the present day.

Every month the Markham Museum and Heritage Village pays tribute to the history of the local area with special community events like the Heritage Festival, Family Day, and Applefest, which is a celebration of the annual harvest. At one time, of course, the harvest was the event of the year.

If visitors want to get an actual taste of life in earlier days, the museum grounds include a Mennonite farmhouse from the 1820s, a caboose of 1940s vintage, and an entire 10-hectare village from days gone by. The Markham Museum is located on Highway 48 just north of 16th Avenue and is conveniently only 20 minutes from major highways and Toronto.

One of the most attractive qualities about Markham is that as it becomes a larger and, in some places, even a bustling urban centre, it still maintains a small-town feel. The Community Gardens Project is indicative of this type of thing. The York Region Food Network and the Town of Markham have worked together to make garden plots available—at no charge! It's strictly first come, first served.

The Markham Pathways Project, another good example of the strong sense of community here, represents 15 kilometres of nature pathways. Indeed, living in Markham means you don't always have to drive. The routes will take you through all the beautiful parklands of the area, including Pomona Mills Park, Milne Dam Conservation Park, Toogood Pond, German Settlers' Park, and even the handsome grounds of the Markham Civic Centre. And, of course, much of Rouge Park, the largest urban park in North America, is in Markham as well. In its entirety, Rouge Park contains more than 4,640 hectares of woodlands, valleys, meadows and farmland.

The Markham Pathways Project is a successful community-wide campaign that helps to ensure that the area's beautiful parklands are maintained. Photo: Benjamin Rondel.

The pathways are wonderful places to enjoy the trees and wildflowers, perch yourself on one of 16 bridges, or watch the birds. Most of the pathways follow creeks and waterways, and any first-time visitor will be immediately struck by the beauty and cleanliness of these meticulous trails. One of the reasons for this enviable state of affairs is that any community group is free to "adopt" a path. That's right. The Town will gladly install a marker with the group's name on it, provided that members act as "pathway ambassadors." This requires keeping the path free of litter, reporting any vandalism, and notifying the municipality of any area that requires maintenance.

Markham's bountiful collection of green space includes almost 2,000 hectares of public parks, baseball diamonds galore, soccer pitches, two cricket pitches, and a rugby pitch! In the true spirit of Markham, there are first-class programs available for those who wish to learn new recreational activities or improve on their skills. The Town offers baseball camps for aspiring major leaguers and outdoor day camps for children as young as four.

Golf and tennis are popular summer sports, and the Town has organized clinics for people of all ages. And the facilities here are recognized for their excellence. For example, the local Angus Glen Golf Club was recently selected as the number one new course in all of Canada by *Golf Digest* magazine. Markham also has a "golf for children" program available at the Unionville Golf Centre on Main Street.

The Markham Guild of Village Crafts offers courses for all ages. In addition to an art camp and a calligraphy course for children, adult courses are available in such pursuits as decorative folk art, pottery, pergamano, and even log cabin renovations. A complete schedule of year-round fitness classes is also popular, as are specialty programs for such sports as canoe and kayak sprint racing or gymnastics. For the technologically inclined, there is a course called "kids and computers."

Markham administers itself in a manner that is typical of the people who live here. In a nutshell, core values are stressed. There is no department called "Parks and Recreation." Instead, a department called "Recreation and Culture" looks after just that—those resources and facilities which involve recreational and cultural pursuits. Parks are administered through "Environmental Services" and waste through "Street Services."

"I think Markham has always been a little bit ahead," says Barbara Roth, Director of Recreation at the Town of Markham. "We got our theatre because this kind of thing is important to the people here. And even the theatre is run with a strong concern about the bottom line. The town is very concerned about being fiscally responsible. As a matter of fact, in our area of recreation and culture, we manage to recover 75 per cent of our total costs, and that's extremely high. But this is how the community is run."

Offering the best of services that are delivered with sound fiscal responsibility, Markham has a mission for its Recreation and Culture program: "To provide leisure, education and entertainment in a safe and cost-effective manner to all customers so that they enjoy the benefits of developing a healthy lifestyle."

Planning for future needs is important to Markham. The town's Master Plan ensures that all recreational-type needs are met. That means ice rinks, soccer fields, ample parkland, you name it. But it also looks at swimming pools, libraries, heritage facilities like museums and historic buildings, and, of course, the arts. It's a complete way of life, and all these things are important to the people of Markham.

The municipal building embodies what the town is all about. While some other municipalities of the GTA have erected huge, sprawling civic centre complexes, Markham's is nothing of the kind. It is a low-level, and low-key, style of building with names perched atop each of the entranceways. What's more, these names haven't been chosen lightly. One of the entrances is called Thornhill. Another is Milliken. Another still is Unionville. All these communities are part of the modern Markham, but each is also strong and distinct in its own right. And so, while an affluent Markham embraces the future with great hope and promise, it isn't so bold that it forgets its beginnings. *m*

The Kathleen Gormley McKay Art Centre, named for the generous sponsor of Frederick Horsman Varley, is located in the former McKay home and serves as a venue for art classes and for exhibitions by local artists.
Photo: Benjamin Rondel.

Chapter Seven

A Legacy of Caring
❖ ❖ ❖
Health Care and Education

*I*f you had to choose one characteristic that has prevailed in Markham since the town's pioneer days, it's a strong sense of community. Consider the life of Josephus Reesor, born in Markham in 1820. He made quite a name for himself as a physician and a herbalist who treated cancer patients. He was, by all accounts, the epitome of the friendly neighbourhood doctor. He continued to provide compassionate care for his patients until his death in 1916. His legacy of caring lives on today in Markham's local hospitals and health care facilities, and in the many social service agencies that reach out to those in need.

In terms of health care, the words "world class" certainly apply to Markham. This sense of quality starts with the two hospitals—Markham Stouffville Hospital, which opened in 1990, and the older Shouldice Hospital, which is a private facility in Thornhill. Both are highly regarded, award-winning institutions.

Markham Stouffville Hospital was built out of necessity; in the 1980s Markham had begun to experience dynamic growth, and it became obvious that a community hospital was needed. It was not long before this facility made its mark. In 1994, just four years after its inception, the 214-bed institution received the highest award from the Canadian Council in Health Service Accreditation, placing it among a select group of hospitals in Canada. A year later it became the first hospital in the country to

Photo: Alan Marsh

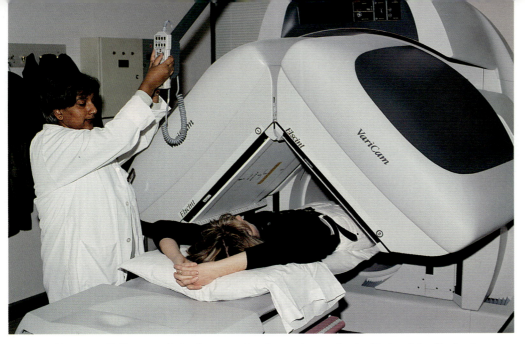

Markham Stouffville Hospital, the first Canadian hospital to receive the National Quality Institute Award for Excellence in Quality Health Care, utilizes a management structure focused on patient needs.
Photo: Markham Stouffville Hospital.

receive the National Quality Institute Award for Excellence in the category of Quality Health Care. These awards are given for excellence shown by corporations, government and education and health care organizations. What's so special about Markham Stouffville Hospital?

"We are quite innovative and progressive in management and in our leadership style," said Rosalie Penny, coordinator of Quality and Customer Relations, which, in itself, is a rather unusual title for a hospital employee. But Markham Stouffville is an unusual hospital. Take its mission statement: "To make every patient's visit a great experience."

Everyone in the hospital, beginning with the president, personally works toward this mission. Even world-renowned management guru Tom Peters was compelled to quote the mission statement in a book of his.

As one of three hospitals in York Region, but the only one in Markham, Markham Stouffville Hospital has about 900 employees and 700 volunteers, which shows tremendous community involvement. And the community has been there from the beginning, when millions of dollars were raised via local fund-raising events such as musical benefits and garage sales in order to help finance the institution.

Today, programs at the hospital are family-centred and patient-focused, hence the focus on "quality." When the hospital won its excellence award, it was praised for creating close ties with local health and social service agencies, a management structure focused on patient needs, and active employee involvement in all levels of planning.

Among its specialties are a Pediatric Diabetes Clinic and a Child and Adolescent Family Service Clinic. If this seems like a lot of attention given to young people, it is. Markham is a young community. In fact, the hospital's Childbirth and Children's Centre deliveries reached 10,000 in February 1996, not quite six years after opening.

But Markham Stouffville Hospital isn't the only health care facility on the premises. Also sitting on the rambling 20-hectare site at the Ninth Line and Highway 7 is a separate Health Centre building housing offices for doctors and specialists, an ambulance station, and Participation House. Participation House, which opened in 1972, is a project of the Cerebral Palsy Parent Council of Toronto. In addition to providing a permanent residence for disabled adults, it provides day care, physiotherapy, recreational activities and life skills development programs.

Like Markham Stouffville Hospital and Participation House, Shouldice Hospital in Thornhill has garnered more than its fair share of acclaim. In fact, you could even say that it's world-famous.

During the Second World War, Dr. Edward Earle Shouldice, a major in the Canadian Army, found that many men couldn't enlist because they needed hernia surgery. He performed an innovative method of surgery on 70 of them so they could join the cause. After the war, he opened his own hospital devoted to hernias. In 1953 he purchased a country estate in a beautiful, picturesque part of Thornhill, and it eventually became an 89-bed facility.

In half a century, surgeons at Shouldice Hospital have performed some

250,000 hernia operations on patients as young as four months and as old as 100 years. What's more, the success rate is greater than 99 per cent! When this institution started, the average hospital stay for hernia surgery was three weeks; at Shouldice, patients walk out of the operating room, stay two or three days, and are usually back at work in a week. It's no surprise that patients and doctors from virtually all over the world have come to this remarkable hospital.

Major health care institutions aside, the spirit of community sharing and community involvement truly permeate all aspects of health care in Markham. The York Region District Health Council, a health care planning body that reports to the Ontario Ministry of Health, is responsible for all of York Region, including Markham. There is sometimes a fine line between health care and social service, so the many health-oriented and social service agencies in the area have joined forces to build a huge Web site database offering just about every type of service and program imaginable.

Markham has its public health inspectors who monitor both sanitary and safety conditions in public and private buildings, a growing Home Care program, which provides an alternative to hospitalization, and special services like the Markham Mobility Bus, which is a transportation service designed for people who are unable to walk or climb stairs. Then there is the Markham Neighbourhood Support Centre, which initiates and coordinates services in response to community need.

And there is more. The Markham Physiotherapy Clinic on Church Street looks at sports injuries and arthritis. There are excellent facilities for senior citizens like the Glynnwood Retirement Residence on Bayview Avenue in Thornhill and Markhaven Incorporated, which is a 75-bed facility on Parkway Avenue. And, of course, there is the umbrella United Way of York Region, which has offices in Markham and which collects funds for many different social service agencies.

The local education system in Markham also has a strong history of building bridges to the community. The earliest school, Markham Village Grammar School, was erected in 1837. In 1871, it became Markham's first high school. For a great many years, Markham High School, which was eventually renamed Markham District High School, was the only public school east of Bayview Avenue. But that changed with the population boom that began in the 1980s.

Yet, the history of education in Markham has not been forgotten. The "Heritage Schoolhouse," a one-room schoolhouse that was built in 1872, has been fully renovated, complete with the original floor, desks and blackboard. Students from local schools often visit to learn about the past.

Today, the York Region District School Board and York Region Catholic District School Board are the two education systems that provide for Markham.

Markham today has many secondary and elementary schools to serve its large student population, and organization is the key. The Markham area comprises the Community Education Centre "East" District, which is one of four districts in the massive area served by the York Region Board of Education. This board works closely with the York Region Catholic District School

The Markham Mobility Bus provides a transportation service designed for those unable to walk or climb stairs. Photo: Benjamin Rondel.

Shaping a Destiny 57

Bill Carothers, chair of the York Region District Board of Education, one of two school systems in Markham. Photo: Benjamin Rondel.

Board. The two boards have shared audio-visual classroom services for over 20 years and, since 1978, they have worked with the Lake Simcoe Conservation Authority to bring outdoor education to students. In 1994, the two boards established the Joint Board Consortium, consisting of their trustees and staff; this is a very successful cooperative effort providing for joint tendering and provision of such services as purchasing, planning, parenting courses, and plant maintenance, which involves everything from snow plow removal to relocating portables. Also in 1994, the two boards implemented a joint student busing service.

In addition to quality elementary and high schools, Markham has countless programs designed to meet special community needs. Many students from grade one through high school are enrolled in French Immersion programs. A popular Continuing Education program offers night school and summer school courses for everything from Driver Education to Language Instruction for Newcomers to Canada. There is also an Adult Basic Literacy program to help adults acquire basic mathematics and language skills, and the increasingly popular business training program in which local educators offer staff development, retraining, and continuous improvement programs to local companies.

Perhaps it's because of the large numbers of students in the area, but schools in Markham are unique in both their high degree of community involvement and their links to the business sector. It is not unusual for local companies to sponsor special events and offer to lend a helping hand.

For example, in 1997, the FIRST Robotics Championship was held; this was a Canada-wide competition challenging schools to build robots which play a modified version of basketball. A team from Unionville High School came away with the top prize in the inaugural competition, as 35 students and two teacher-advisors spent seven weeks on the project. What's more, Motorola of Canada not only sponsored the team, which was called "Wolfpack," but several members of the company's staff also volunteered their time as mentors to the students, providing technical assistance in the construction of the robot. The resulting win proved this was time well spent.

Then there was the Unico Bridge Fair. Sponsored by Unico Foods, this pilot project involved students in grades four to eight at William Berczy Public School. Student teams worked together to set up small companies for the purpose of constructing bridges. The project was so successful that the school and company won the York Region Board of Education's Partnership Award.

What do young people learn about the world of finance and investing? Well, when Ashley Mound was in grade four at Unionville Public School, she showed that she was a budding investment advisor; in a contest

The York Region Catholic District School Board works closely with the York Region District School Board on matters of classroom services, purchasing, planning and more.
Photo: Benjamin Rondel.

58 Shaping A Destiny

sponsored by the *Toronto Star*, she built an imaginary portfolio and saw it grow from $100,000 to more than $170,000—and that was in just three months! Ashley won $10,000 in actual cash for her efforts.

Not only do Markham students win awards, but so do their teachers. In another notable "first" for the community, the principal at William Berczy Public School in Unionville was the first recipient of the Learning Partnership's Charlie Pilksticker Leadership Award for "initiating, developing, and implementing partnership projects that benefit students, schools, and the community." The principal, Helen Gaidatsis, built many bonds between the school and local businesses; examples include the proprietor of a local art gallery teaching students about the history of the Group of Seven, and an engineer guiding students in a poster contest about building techniques.

Winning awards is nothing new for Markham teachers. Carl Twiddy, head of science at Markham District High School, won the Prime Minister's Award for Teaching Excellence in Science, Technology and Mathematics. A long-time pioneer in education, Twiddy developed independent study projects years before they became a requirement for senior high school students. He also established the Industrial Mentorship Program with local chemical industries, and developed co-op classes in biology, chemistry and physics. In addition, he helped launch his school's partnership program with Markham Stouffville Hospital in which the hospital is used as a learning facility.

Likewise, Andy Cherkas, a chemistry and math teacher at Stouffville District High School, won a similar award for his novel approach to teaching science; his Society of Bubbleology Club was an integrated approach to science, mathematics and art, and helped inspire the interest of many female students.

The bond with business is strengthened through an annual project called "Take Our Kids to Work," which allows students in grade nine to accompany their parents for a day at their place of work. Many Markham businesses are happy to participate in this unique program, which takes place throughout the Greater Toronto Area and across Canada.

But making young people responsible citizens involves more than teaching them about business. Markham also has some enlightening programs that teach about the environment. When undergoing a landscape transformation, Unionville Public School thought it best to involve its 575 students. In observing School Yard Day, an annual celebration to establish school yards as vital and dynamic outdoor classrooms, the students were busy planting trees. What's more, local landscapers and arborists donated trees, plants and shrubs. Even the mayor was involved!

Yes, that strong sense of community and caring which began in Markham's pioneer days has definitely prevailed. Today, that legacy lives on in such institutions and services as Markham Stouffville Hospital, Participation House, and Shouldice Hospital, the Markham Mobility Bus and the schools.

The Robotics Championship, first held in 1997, is a Canada-wide competition for the schools. A Unionville High School team, with corporate sponsorship by Motorola, won first prize that year. Photo courtesy Unionville High School.

Built in 1872, the Heritage Schoolhouse is a one-room schoolhouse that has been fully renovated, complete with original floor, desks and blackboard. Below, Allen Meyer, one of the school's former teachers, participates in a class reunion.
Photos: Benjamin Rondel.

Kids of all ages enjoy Markham's many parks and green spaces.
Photos: Benjamin Rondel.

Shaping A Destiny 61

Part II

Chapter Eight

The Business Community
❖ ❖ ❖

Markham Board of Trade 64-65

Craig Riley's Markville Lincoln Mercury 66-67

TD Financial Group 68

Ceridian Canada Ltd. 69

Town of Markham 70-71

BridgeStreet Accommodations 72

V.V. DeMarco Properties, Limited 73

JJ Barnicke Limited 74

Toronto Airways Ltd. 75

Photo: First Light

For the members of the Markham Board of Trade, breakfast means a whole lot more than simply a danish and coffee. The focus is on networking—much of which is achieved at monthly breakfast meetings.

After a full, served breakfast and over morning coffee, everyone in the room has an opportunity to stand up and introduce his or her business, and each business has the option to display brochures and literature in the reception area.

Markham Board of Trade

According to regular attendee Lorne Soehner, of Soehner Displays & Exhibits Inc., "Networking really does work."

Luncheons also are prime opportunities for advancing board members' networking goals. What's more, the MBT annually hosts business-after-hours functions, member open houses, ski and tennis days and a golf tournament, all with a view to providing a relaxed environment for networking. And members are invited to an annual awards dinner at which six Markham businesses are recognized for their business excellence and success.

In 1998, the board launched Markham's first Internet Worldwide Trade Show, a unique opportunity for members to promote their goods and services to more than a million local users and millions more worldwide.

Operating as a non-profit organization under the Boards of Trade Act, the MBT exists to fulfill a twofold function, explains Ruth Burkholder, the board's president and CEO. In addition to facilitating networking opportunities, it lobbies all levels of government on behalf of its members and the business community. Federally, the MBT has lobbied on issues including employer health tax, debt, and the deficit. Provincially, it has made its voice heard regarding the Greater Toronto Services Board and Ontario business taxes. Locally, the board has voiced its views to the Town of Markham on issues such as signage and taxes. Explains Burkholder: "It's important that we represent the business community to all levels of government, for if legislation is put in place that adversely impacts the business community, the economy may slide downward, creating an unstable business environment and a potential increase in unemployment."

CEO Ruth Burkholder and Chair Robert Kiefer launch the MBT's promotional campaign.

MBT luncheon

Originally, the board was launched by a group of business people with an interest in creating an organization to help people do business together, and maintain a strong and healthy business environment. By mid-1998, the MBT comprised 850 company members. Among Ontario's 275 boards of trade and chambers of commerce, the MBT ranks as number 16. "Growth," says Burkholder, "has been steady." More than 90 per cent of MBT members are small businesses with fewer than 50 employees. Members include representatives from all facets of local business life, including legal counsel, accounting, banking, high-tech, insurance, manufacturing, and importing/exporting. IBM, Apple Canada, Allstate and ATI are among some of the well-known corporate names filling out the membership list.

As for the future, the board's direction is clear. "Our plan is to continue to grow," Burkholder says. "The more members we have, the more opportunity they have to do business with one another. And the larger we are, the more clout we will have with government." To that end, the MBT has developed a strategic management plan that targets growth for the organization among the 7,200 Markham-based companies that have not yet joined the board.

Annual membership costs between $210 and $1,300, depending on the size of the company. Members are listed free in the MBT's annual business directory and buyers' guide. They also receive a complimentary listing on the board's Web site, and have free use of the MBT boardroom.

Members are invited to save money by joining the MBT's group insurance plan, by accessing its member discounts and by taking advantage of discounted rates for MasterCard and Visa.

In addition to being a board of trade, the MBT is also recognized as the Markham Chamber of Commerce. It is a member of, and is affiliated with, the Ontario and Canadian chambers of commerce. In 1996, the MBT signed a Memorandum of Understanding with the Scarborough York Region Chinese Business Association, the first in the history of Ontario, thereby partnering their programs and services in order to help mainstream and Chinese businesses do business, and understand each other's culture. The MBT builds relationships within and beyond its membership through 12 committees: government affairs & international trade, marketing, annual awards, breakfast networking, seminar, member open-house, business-after-hours, golf tournament, ski day, tennis tournament, membership development and sales, and membership satisfaction and retention committees.

Breakfast Networking Club meets monthly.

Active networking produces sales.

Among area boards of trade, the MBT is unique in its commitment to networking. Thanks to its more than 100 volunteers, the MBT is able to implement more programs, services, functions and events than any neighboring board of trade or chamber of commerce. Its decision-makers are the 14 directors nominated and elected from within the business community. They make policy decisions on how the board operates, create the vision for the organization's future, and are responsible to the membership.

"We're here to help our businesses grow and gain financial strength," Burkholder explains. "It's our job to make sure the economy stays vibrant, and it's important to maintain an organization that has the clout to influence government decision-making."

Burkholder firmly believes that all businesses can benefit from the assistance of boards of trade and chambers of commerce, and it's a belief that she and the MBT are set on spreading to the four corners of the town of Markham.

Within a sea of Windstars, Escorts, Navigators and Mystiques, Craig Riley's Markville Lincoln Mercury has built a thriving automobile dealership by checking the marketing currents of the present—without losing sight of the past.

The past is evident immediately upon turning into the 2.5-acre Markham, Ontario property, where the town's tallest and largest Canadian flag proudly flies. Here, a heritage log cabin stands at the centre of Markville's pre-owned car

Craig Riley's Markville Lincoln Mercury

division. Fully renovated and refurnished, the 1920s-era structure enables the company to keep in touch with its Unionville roots—a reference to the historic community that comprises Markham.

Since 1993, Markville Lincoln Mercury has been Canada's top seller of Windstar and Villager minivans.

For its part, progress is evident throughout the dealership, most notably in the high-tech training and diagnostic equipment in which Markville has invested. As President Craig Riley explains, the Ford Star System enables Markville technicians and sales staff to upgrade their skills "on site" through interactive training with satellite television.

In addition, the Service Bay Diagnostic System allows Markville technicians to monitor a car's performance remotely, through a mobile system that is then plugged back into their own computers. Adds Riley: "All of this is an advanced technical part of the business that many people aren't aware of. This system helps us diagnose those annoying intermittent problems, and fix the car right, the first time."

From the time the company was launched in 1991, Markville Lincoln Mercury has surpassed expectations. For example, the dealership sells about 1,200 new units annually—double the 600 units anticipated by Ford of Canada. Since 1991, annual sales have quadrupled to $60 million from $15 million. Over the same period, employment has tripled to 60, and the premises have doubled in size.

In addition, Markville has won the Chairman's Award, twice: Ford's most prestigious award, granted to just five per cent of dealers. It has also won the company's Distinguished Achievement Award for Quality, four times: awarded for vehicle sales volume and customer satisfaction.

From 1993 to 1997, Markville was Canada's number one retailer of Windstars and Villagers. Windstar was the first minivan to earn a five-star distinction, the highest U.S. government rating, for the safety of the driver and front passenger in a front-end collision. At least 40 per cent of its annual unit sales volume is minivans.

Located on a one-hectare property in Markham, Ontario, Markville Lincoln Mercury sells about 1,200 new Ford and Lincoln Mercury vehicles annually.

President Craig Riley and his team of 60 believe in "giving back to the community" by supporting local theatre, sports teams and charitable events.

Markville's exemplary results might be credited to its place in the community, and the care it takes to remain a vital part of it. At the Markham Theatre, for example, the company sponsors the Craig Riley's Markville Lincoln Mercury Theatre Series, which includes plays such as *Driving Miss Daisy* and *Ain't Misbehavin'*. Markville is a member of the Markham Board of Trade and supports local soccer, baseball, hockey and synchronized swimming teams.

Markville regularly hosts free community autograph sessions with sports celebrities, such as ex-Toronto Blue Jay Pat Borders and ex-Toronto Raptors star Damon Stoudamire. The dealership also supplies vehicles as hole-in-one giveaways at local and charity-related golf tournaments, including the Scott Goodyear's Easter Seal Society, Town of Markham, Markham-Stouffville Hospital and Metro Ambulance events.

"These initiatives give us a chance to give back to the community," Riley explains. "We're a relatively young business, and we're trying to create an awareness for our dealership by letting people know we're involved in the community. That's important to us as a company."

Progressive dealerships like Markville have radically changed the business of car sales.

"Today's consumer is educated and expects service. We try to exceed our customers' expectations," he says. "The old school tried to close the sale on the spot, but our staff makes no demands on first-time visitors to the showroom. As product advisors, we attempt to gain our customers' confidence so they'll have a reason to come back. We also recognize the influence women have in the car-buying decision. Eighty per cent of all vehicle purchases are influenced by women."

At Markville Lincoln Mercury, staff training and service diagnostics are state of the art.

Markville's ambitions find an excellent home in Markham. "Markham has one of Canada's highest per-capita earnings rates," Riley says. "Plus, it's a growing community, with a reasonably low tax base and a supportive mayor and council. Property values have been retained through the recession, so any investment in land and buildings is not just a capital expense, it's more of a capital investment. Markham is the perfect place for progressive businesses."

The first Toronto Dominion Bank branch in Markham opened in 1959, four years after the amalgamation of the Bank of Toronto and the Dominion Bank. Nearly 40 years later, despite the tremendous changes Markham has experienced, that same branch—in the Markham Shopping Centre—is still going strong. And a whole "bank culture" has grown up around it. TD Financial Group, comprised of TD Bank and its subsidiaries, employs over 700 people in Markham.

TD Financial Group

Proud to Play a Role in Markham's Success

TD's first branch in Markham, opened in 1959 as it appears today.

For two years in a row, TD has been ranked number one in a national survey comparing the quality of mutual fund investment advice and service among financial institutions.
An independent survey conducted by Marketing Solutions.

When you go into any TD branch in Markham, you will see, on a poster or on a brochure, the phrase: "We're here to help make it easier." These words speak volumes about TD's culture, attitude, and strategies. They are TD's commitment to its customers: to help make their financial lives easier by providing them with the products and services they want, by offering advice in managing their financial affairs and by delivering these services as simply, conveniently and cost-effectively as possible.

TD Bank Financial Group plays a variety of roles for people and businesses from its two major commercial centres and six retail outlets serving Markham. For individual investors, TD's wealth management services help make it easier to invest through discount and full service brokerages, mutual funds, or trust services. For consumers, TD Access has a full range of electronic delivery options. TD branches offer many other personal services, for example, currency exchange. For Markham's business clients, TD offers commercial banking services with key areas of specialization adapted to local needs.

In 1992, TD established its first Technology Banking Centre in Markham, at Woodbine and Steeles. One of the first of its kind in Canada, the Technology Banking Centre specializes in serving the unique needs of high-technology companies—a significant part of Markham's economy.

TD is also making banking easier for Markham's substantial Asian community by employing multilingual staff at every branch to help Asian customers make a smooth transition to life in Canada.

Markham has undergone amazing growth in recent years. To meet the needs of its customers, TD has specialized, especially at the Beaver Creek location, in providing real estate financing to developers and builders.

To make it easier for small businesses to manage their financial affairs, TD introduced its Main$treet Banking program, which will deliver commercial services at every TD branch, enabling owner-managers to do their banking near their business with a banker who understands their business.

The key to these initiatives is relationship banking—building a genuine rapport with customers—which allows TD bankers to better understand its customers and their businesses—and to deliver products and services to help make it easier for its customers to meet their financial needs and goals.

TD Bank Financial Group is proud of the strong relationships it has developed with the people of Markham. And TD has enjoyed the opportunity to be part of the continuing growth and development of this great community as it celebrates the achievements of the past and prepares for success in the future.

Ceridian Canada Ltd. is a recent acquisition of Ceridian Corporation, a global leader in information services for the human resource, electronic media and transportation industries. Concentrated in the payroll and human resource management systems (HRMS) business, Ceridian Canada Ltd. combines the experience and knowledge of CIBC/Comcheq and TD Payroll & HR Solutions to create Canada's leading payroll company.

Ceridian Canada Ltd.

Ceridian Canada offers a range of products and services tailored to meet the varying needs of its clients. Ceridian Canada account representatives handle customer inquiries personally and develop relationships with clients and a familiarity with their payroll processing operations and requirements.

For owner-managers of small businesses, time and accuracy are the most important factors in making sure their employees get paid. Ceridian Canada business solutions, based on telephone or fax input of payroll information, make the process as quick and simple as possible. Another important aspect of Ceridian Canada's service is remitting of statutory deductions to the proper government bodies. Remitting can be both time-consuming and expensive if handled improperly, so making sure it's done right is just part of the service.

For mid- and large-sized customers, Ceridian Canada offers PC-based solutions which feature the user-friendly Windows™ environment. Customers transmit files containing their up-to-date payroll information from their PC to Ceridian Canada for processing. As a result, the customer has complete control over employee information and can take advantage of powerful system maintenance, update and report writing capabilities. Customers also have the option of having their employees' pay deposited directly into an account at any Canadian financial institution. These Ceridian Canada programs, developed to meet the specific needs of customers, ensure accurate and timely processing of payrolls, which leaves the owner/manager more time to take care of business.

Ceridian Canada's PC-based solutions feature the user-friendly Windows™ environment.

In addition to payroll processing, Ceridian Canada's systems act as a link between employees and certain group savings plans. A group savings plan helps employees save for retirement—and get immediate tax relief—by selecting from a variety of investment options with amounts deducted directly from their pay. It's the easy way to pay yourself first.

After 65 years of running payrolls and remitting taxes in the U.S., Ceridian Corp. has moved north of the border to take service excellence to the next level and give customers more than what they expect. Ceridian Canada Ltd.'s focus is on achieving exceptional customer service through innovative products and services. It plans to lead the payroll industry into the next millennium of growth and beyond.

Professional customer training is one of the many value-added services that Ceridian Canada offers.

The Town of Markham is the place to be for many people. It's a successful and admired community of cultures and opportunities with a wonderful atmosphere for raising a family. As Canada's "High-Tech Capital," it's the perfect base for technology companies. But, whether private or corporate citizen, everybody who resides here is proud to call Markham "home."

Town of Markham

Markham's population is about 190,000 and growing. Here, the Canadian dream of owning a home in a high-quality neighborhood can be fully realized. For families, Markham boasts 34 elementary schools, 7 secondary schools, 20 elementary and 9 secondary separate schools, 43 daycare centres and nursery schools, and 2 day camps.

Embassy Suites

And residents can take advantage of the award-winning development taking place here. In 1997, the Ontario Homebuilders Association voted Angus Glen one of the best new home developments. Cornell, another award-winning development expected to unfold over 20 years, introduces the philosophy of new urbanism to the area.

Markham's community-based approach to living emphasizes neighborhood identity, recreational facilities and pedestrian access. New urbanism housing promotes the front porch and rear garage models that defined finer neighbourhoods in former years. Houses are set close to tight grids of short streets, and within a five-minute walk of typical amenities. Markham is a forerunner among North American municipalities for its efforts in promoting the concept of new urbanism.

Ultimately, Cornell (Markham's flagship new urbanism community) will comprise 10,000 homes in 11 neighbourhoods, each with parks, open spaces, services and 162,000 square metres of office space.

In addition, Markham has been a leader in the area of waste management. The Blue Box recycling program is well entrenched, and the Town is examining other options for more effective garbage disposal, including the possibility of wet and dry garbage collection. The Recycling Council of Ontario recognized Markham's efforts with its gold award in 1991, when 29 per cent of the town's waste was diverted from a landfill. As part of the Rouge River basin, Markham participates in the river's conservation and development. It features bicycle trails and walkways through many ravines. "It's a very ecologically friendly place to be," says Markham's Mayor.

In 1997, Markham won the Communities in Bloom award, granted by a national organization that judges communities across Canada on criteria including community involvement, landscaping, beauty of flowers and grassy areas, and environmental effort.

Allstate Building

Unionville Festival - One of many annual community celebrations in Markham

Markham is a proud and prosperous town. People who live and work in Markham have some of Ontario's highest income levels. There's a keen sense of neighbourhood, with excellent schools and enthusiastic teachers, chic boutiques and antique shops, regional shopping centres, big-box discount retailers, cinemas, libraries, parks and protected natural features. The Mayor talks about Markham as a town of communities—Thornhill, Markham, Unionville, Milliken Mills and Buttonville—and cosmopolitan neighbourhoods, including sizeable Chinese and South Asian populations. Residents enjoy excellent recreational facilities, such as arenas, a new sports soccer dome, a theatre, an art gallery and an impressive museum, more than 1,600 hectares of parkland and a 15-kilometre pathways system.

An ample supply of shopping and entertainment is already in place and continues to be augmented by new projects such as a 28,800-square-metre shopping centre is under construction on Highway 7 near Warden Ave. Among its features will be a 10-screen Cineplex theatre and Canada's largest Moevenpick Marché restaurant.

For world-class businesses based here—including Nike, Apple Canada, IBM, Liberty Health, American Express, Sun Microsystems and Allstate Insurance—the attractions are many. There's easy access to downtown Toronto and to business centres across the GTA by superhighways 404 and 407. Markham's export-oriented businesses are well served by two international airports: Toronto's Pearson International Airport and the local Toronto Buttonville Municipal Airport. Markham boasts an attractive tax rate; a well-educated labour force; an efficient, business-friendly government; higher-than-average household incomes; and a booming local economy.

What's more, Markham's town council is committed to delivering quality services while keeping costs down. It continues to maintain significantly lower tax rates than the City of Toronto while continuing to deliver top-quality civic services to residents and local businesses.

For a municipality its size, Markham has attracted the largest concentration of high-tech firms in Canada. Markham's multiple fibre-optic access lines, integrated into a national fibre-optic network, provide an unrivalled telecommunications infrastructure, which enables local businesses to move massive amounts of voice communication, data and images at high speeds across that network.

Class A office and industrial buildings in Markham are taxed at rates up to 50 per cent lower than in Toronto. Lease rates are always competitive, all with free parking. Vacant, fully serviced industrial land is available in 15 business parks bounded by Highways 404, 7, 48 and 407. Zoned for varied industrial and commercial uses, land is available for $200,000 to $700,000 per acre, most of it about 20 minutes from Pearson International Airport.

Civic Centre

Shaping a Destiny 71

When you're a business traveller heading out of town for an extended stay, you want your accommodations in order. But where do you stay while in England or Japan, the U.S.A., or, for that matter, Canada, or even Markham?

BridgeStreet Accommodations, formerly Global Travel Apartments, provides furnished corporate housing by the day, week or month in 26 countries and 200 cities around the world.

BridgeStreet Accommodations

BridgeStreet's corporate furnished housing properties are located in several convenient locations throughout Markham and include excellent security, full health club facilities and parking.

Attractive and spacious corporate apartments offer more comfortable and convenient accommodation for the business traveller on an extended stay.

"We provide the comfort, space, convenience and privacy that business travellers look for when relocating, on training or an assignment, at more competitive rates than a hotel room," says Thomas Vincent, President, BridgeStreet Canada.

Besides its own leasehold and managed properties, the company has forged alliances with enterprises throughout the world, who ensure the quality of their furnished corporate housing. As part of this international network, BridgeStreet has over 200,000 corporate housing units in its worldwide inventory.

BridgeStreet Accommodations Inc., a fast-growing U.S. company and top provider of furnished corporate housing, acquired Global Travel Apartments in early 1998. Beyond its rapid expansion across the U.S. and newly established presence in Canada, BridgeStreet intends to establish its own operations throughout Europe and Asia. Its reputation for high quality rests squarely on a solid foundation of superior facilities and services.

"When I started in this unique business I found many business travellers were looking for corporate housing, but when I researched what was available, I found the product wasn't customer-friendly. If I wouldn't stay there myself, why should I expect someone else to? I decided to come up with a better product and service."

BridgeStreet has built an extensive apartment inventory, on its own or through partners, that meets a higher level of service and comfort. Customers can now access a range of suitable accommodations in standard, executive and deluxe qualities, and book their stay through the BridgeStreet central office.

The majority of BridgeStreet's business in Canada is derived from travellers coming to the Greater Toronto Area. The remainder is from people seeking accommodation anywhere else around the globe.

Vincent says BridgeStreet's Markham properties are integral to its housing network. Sites such as Bamburgh Gate provide spacious one- and two-bedroom suites, conveniently located close to shopping and businesses throughout Markham. Additional properties in Markham are already in the planning stage.

"We watch where business is growing, and follow with our product," says Vincent. "Business has grown tremendously in the high-tech and consulting industries in Markham, so there's an enormous demand for our furnished apartments here."

BridgeStreet's extensive World Wide Web site lets people view BridgeStreet's accommodations around the world. They can view colour photos, descriptions and floor plans or take a panoramic virtual tour through the site, and even book their stay immediately on-line.

"Our vision is to remain the number one information source on furnished corporate housing worldwide," says Vincent. With access to 200,000 homes away from home, business travellers know it doesn't matter where they're staying when they use BridgeStreet—they're staying in comfort.

Strung across the head-office walls of V.V. DeMarco Properties, Limited like a necklace of pearls and onyx are photos that tell a multi-layered story. Certainly, it's a story about a Markham, Ontario-based building company and its 50 years of operation. But it's also a story about a community, told silently through the fashion of the structures whose images line the walls.

V.V. DeMarco Properties, Limited

During his first year in business—1946—company founder and chairman Vincent Victor DeMarco built just one home; six years later, he built 150. To date, the company has built more than 1,300 homes. That careful pace is a hallmark of the firm, which has made its name by developing and building quality projects in communities chosen with homeowners in mind.

Today, DeMarco Properties is active in three areas: land development, construction and property management. The balance among them changes with economic conditions; since 1992, for example, the emphasis has been on residential construction. Property management is an area the company seeks to expand.

In an industry known for its competitiveness and high turnover, the longevity of DeMarco Properties is a remarkable accomplishment. President Lawrence DeMarco, the youngest of Vincent's nine children, says the company's track record is a credit to his father's integrity. For example, the senior DeMarco refuses to conduct business through shell, numbered or holding companies. Unlike developers who walk away from projects that sour, DeMarco Properties stands firmly behind its work.

When many builders and developers mortgaged themselves to ride the roller-coaster real estate market over the past 20 years, DeMarco Properties was better positioned to survive. Vincent DeMarco wasn't a man to take on more than he could handle. While some critics might argue that DeMarco missed opportunities when the market was hottest, most observers have grown to respect the conservative approach to financial planning that is the company's credo.

In 1976, DeMarco bought 76 acres (31 hectares) in Markham and relocated his operations and office staff from North York, Ontario, to the town he calls "developmentally progressive and aggressive." Over the years, DeMarco has made a substantial impact on the face of the community. Currently, DeMarco-built properties in Markham include the following: 14 industrial buildings, three residential subdivisions, two commercial projects, and a residential condominium.

Of course, when DeMarco bought the site in what was then a farmer's field, many people thought he was nuts. "But he had a knack for seeing the potential of land," says Lawrence DeMarco. "And look at him now."

The DeMarco Atrium, home of V.V. DeMarco Properties, Limited, earned the town of Markham's Design Achievement Award in 1990.

Located off 14th Avenue in Markham, Ontario, Enclave on the Rouge is V.V. DeMarco's most recent residential subdivision in Markham.

Shaping a Destiny 73

Real Estate giant JJ Barnicke, whose name is recognized worldwide, has recently spread its already expansive wings to comprise a significant presence in Markham, Ontario. Under the direction of Peter Mason, SIOR, FRI, PLE, senior vice-president, JJ Barnicke has merged with Mason International Inc. Realtor to become Barnicke's northeast Greater Toronto Area office. Mason was instrumental to the major growth in the industrial/commercial market in Markham for the past

JJ Barnicke Limited

From left to right: Peter L. Mason, senior vice-president, JJ Barnicke; Don Cousens, mayor of Markham; J.J. Barnicke, chairman

three decades. He was involved in bringing to completion the Scotia Tower, Digital, Pillsbury Towers and the Radisson Hotel at Highway 404 and Highway 7.

In the big picture, Barnicke is the largest independent commercial broker in Canada. It has offices in 20 Canadian cities from Victoria to Halifax, enjoys the support of 49 global partners, serves 30 countries and 200 global business markets and employs nearly 6,000 real estate professionals worldwide. The JJ Barnicke National Group of Companies is a seamless partnership of jointly owned and independent Canadian realty firms that are respected, dominant practitioners in their respective markets.

The company is a major participant in all significant realty sectors, including office, industrial, investment, retail, hospitality and corporate services. Indeed, Barnicke has dominated these sectors in Canada for four decades. The company works for developers, investors, lenders, owners and tenants. It provides advice for any kind of real estate transaction in any market worldwide.

On a local basis, Mason calls Markham "one of few communities where you get a sense of true community, not only from the residents, but from the corporations who've settled here. It's the high-tech capital of Canada. Consequently, it attracts a tremendous amount of business." And it's all business Mason and Barnicke, along with the 40 people who staff the Markham office, are eager to serve.

"With all of our offices across Canada, our ability to draw industry from across the country interested in relocating to Ontario is very powerful," Mason explains. "And one key area we'll highlight is the advantages available in the Town of Markham."

500 Hood Road - One of the quality buildings located in Markham

74 Shaping A Destiny

Outside the hangar, the air sings with the rhapsody of flight. Graceful aircraft sail across the tarmac before catching the breeze and rising over the local neighbourhood of aircraft hangars and corporate headquarters and then off and into the clouds.

This is the Toronto Buttonville Municipal Airport, on the edge of Markham, Ontario and it's a big part of the city's current appeal as the site for new and expanding businesses.

Toronto Airways Ltd.

The Toronto Buttonville Municipal Airport, which was established in the 1950s with a single grass strip and one metal hangar, now boasts four runways and 18 hangars. The airport comprises a full-time customs operation, a flight service weather station, a control tower, aircraft and parts sales businesses, aircraft maintenance operations and a fuel service operation for more than 250 host aircraft and hundreds of itinerant aircraft.

Toronto Airways Ltd. has been the owner and operator of the Toronto Buttonville Municipal Airport since the company was established in 1961. Toronto Airways Ltd. currently employs nearly 100 people, along with another 200 who work for on-site tenants. Along with Toronto Airway's own flight school, which is one of the largest in the country, the Toronto Buttonville Municipal Airport is also home base for three other flight training schools and many Toronto area airborne traffic reporters.

Over the years, the airport has accommodated most corporate jets in modern production. Notable clients include Magna International, Union Gas, American Express, Amway, Leitch Technologies and Exco Technologies. On average, the Toronto Buttonville Municipal Airport receives eight to ten itinerant aircraft daily, arriving from all parts of Canada, the United States and various parts of Europe.

Some years ago, the airport was visited by company executives of Lego who were in Markham from Scandinavia. Soon after the visit, an industrial warehouse with a Lego Corporate sign on it grew out of the ground about two kilometres north of the airport. "If the airport weren't here," reminds Derek Sifton, vice-president of Toronto Airways, "that warehouse probably wouldn't be here, either."

Aerial view of the Toronto Buttonville Municipal Airport, favourably located adjacent to Highway 404.

Toronto Buttonville Municipal Airport competes with Lester B. Pearson International Airport, Toronto City Centre Airport and the Oshawa Airport, all of which are Ontario-based landing strips for corporate business. To make itself more desirable, Sifton explains, his facility aims to provide a high level of service. Indeed, it's the only Canadian facility in MILLION AIR, an international quality-standard aircraft servicing organization recognized by many frequent corporate travellers.

"One of our main attractions is our convenient location," Sifton adds. "We're immediately adjacent to Highway 404, two kilometres north of Highway 407 and minutes from Ontario's main corridor, Highway 401."

"When you compare ours with other facilities, which might be more elaborate but require you to go through a subdivision and a tangle of country roads, ours definitely comes out on top."

One of the airport's many corporate visitors doing business in the local area.

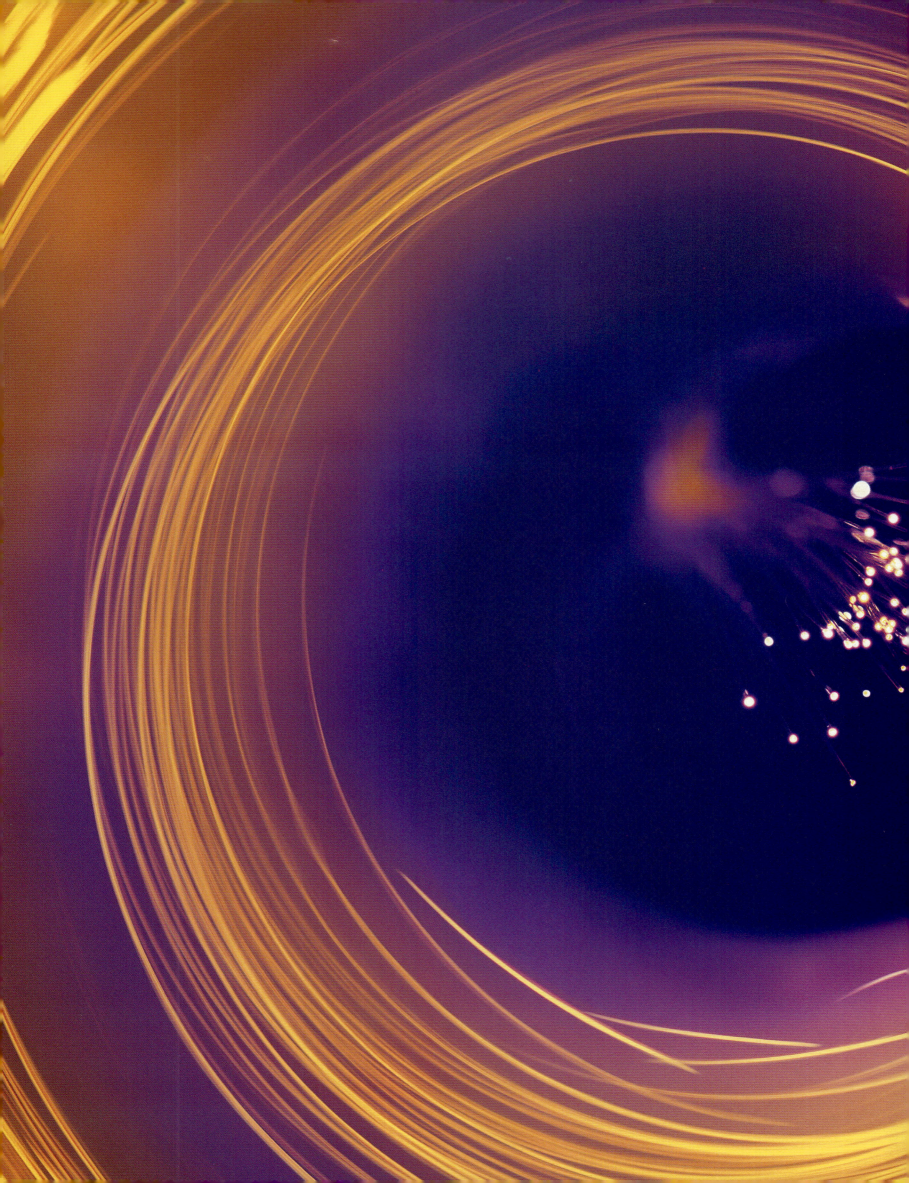

Chapter Nine

High Technology

❖ ❖ ❖

IBM Canada Ltd. 78-79

Comtronic Computers 80

Technica House Canada Inc. 81

GE Multilin 82-83

*Humphrey Fluid
Power Limited 84-85*

Delfour Corporation 86-87

Computron Systems 88

InSystems Technologies 89

Eprom Inc. 90

Jaba System Inc. 91

Photo: First Light

You can always tell where IBM has set up shop, because a blue glow suffuses the local community. That's because Big Blue believes in giving back to the places in which its employees work, live and educate their children—including Markham, site of the Canadian head office.

IBM has been in Canada since 1917, when the Canadian arm became the first foreign subsidiary and the first company to adopt the International Business

IBM Canada Ltd.

Machines name—and the initials IBM. So well known are those three letters today that IBM Canada Ltd. is widely recognized as a leading provider of advanced information technology (IT) products and services.

Since 1992, IBM Canada has been a corporate sponsor of the Professional Entertainment Season at the Markham Theatre for the Performing Arts. The company has also contributed IBM PCs worth $35,000 to run its box-office operations.

IBM Canada has a marketing and service presence in all major cities across Canada, including that provided by a leading-edge manufacturing facility in Bromont, Quebec, and a world-class software-development lab in Don Mills, Ontario. The Markham office has national responsibility for marketing and service, in addition to its sizeable operations in manufacturing, research and development.

In 1997, IBM Canada contributed $1.7 million in cash, equipment and other resources to non-profit and charitable organizations. The information technology leader directs its charitable activities primarily toward organizations in the education, health and welfare fields whose activities benefit Canadian communities.

In 1972, IBM Canada established its Fund for Community Service to encourage and recognize its employees and retirees who serve their communities through non-profit organizations or groups. Canadian non-profit and charitable organizations that perform community-based health, social welfare or civic services in Canada are eligible for consideration.

Meanwhile, IBM Canada gives to its community most directly in the form of employment. In 1997, IBM Canada and its wholly owned subsidiaries hired more than 2,600 people— 5,000 over the past two years. That move brought the company's total Canadian workforce to 15,383—an all-time high. In addition, IBM Canada provided work experience for 500 students and temporary employment to more than 1,966 Canadians.

In an increasingly knowledge-based world, IBM Canada's foremost assets are intellectual capital and the skill of its employees. In 1997, IBM Canada invested $55 million in staff training and education.

In the near term, IBM Canada's strategy is to grow faster than the IT industry as a whole. In 1997, the company's domestic revenues jumped 13 per cent—up to 4 per cent above IT industry levels to a record $4.1 billion.

As part of its corporate strategy to support organizations that assist people with special needs, IBM Canada has given more than $15,000 in technology to Participation House, a Markham, Ontario-based organization that provides homes and personal-care services to disabled adults.

Across Canada, the company is proud of its broader contributions and accomplishments. In addition to job creation, IBM Canada supports the Canadian economy through significant investment, technology transfer, preferred use of Canadian vendors and extensive participation in university research programs. During the 1990s, IBM Canada has invested nearly $2 billion in R&D, making it Canada's third-largest R&D establishment. In 1997, it kept its title as number one IT exporter, with $3.3 billion in exports. IBM Canada is one of the largest suppliers of PCs to the Canadian marketplace, and it ended 1997 with the best customer-service rating in its industry.

Established in 1991, the IBM Canada Centre for Advanced Studies is the leadership model for cooperative research involving industry, academia and governments. Through industry-leading research, students and professors learn first-hand what the industry and customers really need.

In 1972, IBM Canada set up its Fund for Community Service program to encourage and recognize employees, retirees and spouses who serve their communities through non-profit organizations and groups. Organizations such as the Unionville Home Society's Heritage Centre can qualify for corporate donations of cash or technology.

In 1997, IBM coined the phrase e-business to describe the value its customers derive from network computing. More than just the buying and selling of products and services over the Internet, e-business describes how customers are reinventing their business models around network transactions of all kinds—among employees, with suppliers, with business partners and customers.

In the network era, e-business is becomming an even greater facet of everyday life. IBM Canada is set to capitalize on this new reality with a full breadth of hardware, software and service solutions that are unmatched by any other company in the industry. In the past year, IBM has completed thousands of e-business engagements with customers and expects that number to double in 1998.

In an industry noted for its pace of progress, the ability to move quickly is imperative. That might seem a significant challenge for a company the size of IBM Canada, but this IT leader is confident it can react as required. With a reputation for quality, innovation and productivity, IBM Canada is poised to lead the technological charge into the future.

After all, the IT industry values most what IBM does best: it solves customer problems with innovative technology solutions, IBM Canada—big, bright and bustling with the energy of thousands of creative thinkers—is ready to provide those solutions to the community, the country and the world.

The head office of IBM Canada Ltd. is located in this 81,000-square-metre complex in Markham, Ontario.

Comtronic is a national computer distributor providing a wide range of full-system and component solutions. Its impressive line of peripherals from Acer, Brother, Daewoo, Intel, and Western Digital are only a few of the well-known brand name products that Comtronic carries. Comtronic is the exclusive distributor of Zida and the number one distributor of Acer components in Canada. Focused beyond

Comtronic Computers

distribution, Comtronic also specializes in building high-quality systems, backed by complete support services.

Established in 1987 by Mr. John Tse, president of Comtronic, the company has definitely proven its strength among the information technology (IT) community. Within 10 years, the company has expanded its locations across Canada, from British Columbia to Nova Scotia. In Markham, Comtronic occupies a 53,000-square-foot plant which is home to over 100 employees. Its extensive client base in the distribution sector includes over 3,000 resellers, system integrators and retail outlets.

With 10 years of business experience and phenomenal growth that is evident through its expansion of branches, Comtronic is committed to becoming a one-stop solution centre for all its customers' needs. The company's sales revenue has increased from $1 million in its first year to over $200 million for 1998, projected.

Comtronic's rapid growth has created a strong reputation in the IT community. In October 1997, its Markham head office moved to a new site which is located in the heart of the high-end technology area in Ontario.

Comtronic has a business philosophy that works. It concentrates on major industry players in order to share the benefits of a strong vendor-distributor relationship with its customers.

"We make it our business to understand the compatibilities for all the components in a particular brand," explains Elton Lam, marketing manager for Comtronic. As a result, the company invests significant time in researching its line to ensure a family of products that work well together. "If we find these components don't match those peripherals, such as this hard drive doesn't work with that modem, well, we won't choose it."

In October 1997, Comtronic opened its new head office in Markham. Pictured, from left to right: Mayor of Markham, Donald Cousens; Comtronic President, John Tse; Regional Councillor for Markham, Gordon Landon and Minister of Consumer & Commercial Relations, David H. Tsubouchi.

According to Lam, this simple approach means Comtronic has no real competition. As Comtronic operates as a one-stop solution house, it experiences no competition from single-unit suppliers. The company also aims at educating clients, and encourages employees to update customers on industry developments at every turn. Lam says that people often get computer news from unreliable sources, so educating customers about the ever-changing industry is one of its biggest challenges.

Comtronic staff consider it part of their mandate to provide a road map for customers to make informed decisions. Lam notes that their customers appreciate this kind of information. Otherwise, they could end up making costly mistakes—for their budgets and those of their own clients.

Largely a distribution company, Comtronic plans to enhance the scope of its activities by expanding its manufacturing operation. As a result, Comtronic's systems-integration manufacturing operation, which produces house-brand products for small retailers, is to expand significantly. By the end of 1998, Comtronic intends to be in a position to target major global companies.

In Markham, Comtronic occupies a 53,000-square-foot plant which is home to over 100 employees.

Technica House Canada Inc. (CAS) is a company in revolt. But this revolution is unlike one that might erupt in an angry Third World stronghold. Instead, it's a positive move that is seeing this Markham, Ontario-based firm explode into a much larger, more powerful entity.

For a decade, CAS has been in the computer hardware distribution and

Technica House Canada Inc.

assembly business. It has developed a substantial worldwide network for computers, dealing mostly with computer distribution companies, which CAS supplies with everything from memory boards to CPUs. CAS also sells fully manufactured computers from its once-modest manufacturing arm—which is now poised to reap the benefits of the revolt.

In 1997, CAS launched a company called NCCM. That company was set up to serve as the manufacturing heart of CAS; eventually, it is likely to form a company much larger than CAS. From a base in Lewisporte, Newfoundland, NCCM manufactures computers and ships them to CAS customers in the U.S., South America, Romania, Russia and the Middle East.

Meanwhile, the Markham operation oversees all head-office and marketing duties for the 100-person Atlantic unit, while continuing to flourish as a distributor of individual computer parts. In Markham, CAS employs 15 in its 630-square-metre warehouse and 360-square-metre head office just around the corner.

In a sea of computer distributors as deep as it is wide, individual firms are at constant risk of drowning. But CAS has always strived to differentiate itself, particularly through its strong relationships with suppliers and its attention to detail when serving customers. What's more, its abilities to be aggressive, to monitor the marketplace on a daily basis, to buy intelligently and to call on a strong global network have all served it well.

Over the years, customers have learned to rely on CAS products. And if there's a problem, the company is quick to provide service. "We don't leave people in the lurch," says Lou Gallucci, vice-president of corporate development for CAS and NCCM. With the major addition of the cost-effective Newfoundland operation, CAS can produce a high-quality, affordable computer system. Still, Gallucci says, "It all comes down to reputation—and ours is certainly a good one."

Markham has always been able to successfully manage its tremendous natural gifts with ambitious economic development. Photo: Benjamin Rondel.

When General Electric purchased Multilin of Canada in September 1995, it gained a medium-sized company with enormous ideas and goals. GE bought the Markham, Ontario-based firm in an effort to see through on its commitment to be a leader in all of its businesses. Multilin enjoyed an overwhelmingly positive reputation in the motor protection industry in which GE wanted to share.

Indeed, the Multilin name had long been synonymous with good things

GE Multilin

among the major players in North America's power industry. But the benefits of the GE-Multilin marriage were mutual: Multilin was a high-growth company even before it joined the GE family, but its revenues have doubled in the two years since its purchase by GE.

General Electric Multilin, Inc. designs and manufactures microprocessor-based relays that protect and control power systems. These intricate devices find a wide range of uses in four key market segments: generation, including hydro and nuclear plants; transmission, such as power-transmission towers and pole lines; distribution, such as substations that convert high-voltage to lower-voltage forms of power; and industrial end-users, especially substantial power consumers such as petrochemical and pulp and paper companies.

General Electric Multilin Inc. designs and manufactures microprocessor-based relays for the power and control industries in its 7,920-square-metre head office in Markham, Ontario.

GE Multilin products protect people and equipment against damage from over- or under-voltage conditions, undercurrents, short circuits, ground faults or other abnormalities that can occur in the business of generating, transmitting, delivering and consuming power. In effect, the company sells an electronic insurance policy that will, for example, help a client avoid a $30,000 repair bill for a burned-out AC motor thanks to a $2,000 investment in foresight.

In addition to protection, GE Multilin technology offers troubleshooting, analysis and control capabilities through which an operator can wield some control over equipment. "We're primarily in the protection business and our products are becoming more sophisticated as controlling devices," explains Dan McDonnell, GE Multilin's operations manager. "Our customers continue to demand increasing capability and performance and as such, we continually need to enhance our product technology." The goal? Finding broader solutions.

GE Multilin's high-tech products protect people and equipment from unsafe conditions that may occur during the generation and delivery of power.

Multilin began as a three-person operation in Scarborough, Ontario, in 1978 and relocated to Markham in 1980. When GE purchased Multilin, 150 employees occupied 50,000 square feet of space. Currently, GE Multilin employs 197 (and more in summer) in 88,000 square feet of space.

82 Shaping A Destiny

The company is establishing a worldwide distribution network for its world-class products.

What makes GE Multilin unique in a highly competitive industry? Sophisticated technology, leading-edge products, its focus on service and support, its responsiveness, its appreciation of the people behind the products and its flexibility. Says McDonnell: "We don't have just one colour Model T, like some of our competition; our products are designed to meet a full range of needs."

Currently, GE Multilin is establishing distribution channels worldwide and developing a world-class manufacturing process. "This process is something most manufacturers talk about in vague terms," McDonnell explains. "To us, it means being an agile, fast and flexible manufacturer."

If such goals seem within reach, all credit is due to the company's well-respected workforce. According to McDonnell, the GE Multilin philosophy values self-management and wide-ranging staff empowerment. Employees are encouraged to excel and to strive for the opportunities that lie within reach. The line between staff and management is intentionally fuzzy, and all employees are encouraged to engage in "management tasks," such as scheduling and planning, regardless of their official level in the company.

When it comes to furnishing its manufacturing efforts, GE Multilin regularly calls on local subcontractors. Indeed, Markham-based suppliers of electronic components, magnetics, packaging materials, circuit boards and many other products and services are integral to the company's success.

GE Multilin pays recognition to the town that offers a strong high-tech infrastructure, talented workforce and reasonable tax base through its support for Earth Day projects, the local blood bank and community sports events.

Plans include a continued emphasis on new technology, ensuring that GE Multilin products will always be regarded as "the next generation." The company is also working on a platform-based family of products with a "complete package" look and feel. Adds McDonnell: "Whoever can offer a capable, user-friendly 'total solution' that provides the most value will win in the end."

At GE Multilin, self-management and empowerment are key watchwords for employees at all levels.

Most people try to avoid pressure at work; not the people at Humphrey Fluid Power Limited—pressure is the raison d'être of the operation. Humphrey is a leader in the manufacturing of pneumatic components—the industry organized around those pieces of equipment using compressed air to automate manufacturing, medical and other tasks.

Humphrey Fluid Power Limited

Humphrey's Customer Service Group focuses on providing outstanding service to every caller.

The Humphrey warehouse in Markham, Ontario, was officially opened in May 1988 with fewer than 1,000 products. Ten years later, it houses more than 4,000 different products.

Humphrey provides the compressed air (pneumatic) components—valves, actuators, and other accessories—which, together, serve as the "nerves" and "muscles" of production machinery, and provide movement, such as a robot might do. Computers and other controlling devices such as programmable logic controllers usually serve as the "brain" on this type of equipment. Pneumatics, married with electronics, provide many solutions to today's manufacturing challenges.

In essence, Humphrey's products help to automate both routine and complicated operations. Its products help reduce the labour content and cost of manufacturing, improve the productivity of the manufacturing process and increase profitability.

Humphrey's key markets include the automotive, transportation, conveyor, packaging, semiconductor and medical industries. Applications for Humphrey products range from the mundane to the miraculous. For example, Humphrey valves and actuators help automate candy wrapping, mass-producing blue jeans stitchers, and packaging cereal. Car, truck and sport utility vehicle assembly lines use Humphrey's pneumatic components in making car seats, window operators, and other assemblies. Automated milking machines get a hand from Humphrey valves. Water pumps on fire trucks, safety devices and retractable signs on school buses, and NASA booster tanks propelling the space shuttles are all driven in part by compressed air flowing through Humphrey products. You can find Humphrey components on medical breathing apparatus such as respirators and oxygen concentrators, as well as on automated hospital beds. Even the first artificial heart was controlled by dependable Humphrey valves.

Humphrey Fluid Power Limited was established in Markham, Ontario, as a sales office in 1986, and in 1988 opened its warehouse here. Its Kalamazoo, Michigan-based parent, Humphrey Products Company, was launched in 1901. (Markham is Humphrey's only branch office, although it has several subsidiaries.) The parent company, together with its (30-year strong) strategic ally in Japan does the manufacturing, and Markham provides sales, marketing and distribution for Canada.

In Canada, Humphrey employs 11 people; in the U.S., its workforce numbers more than 400. The company also enjoys its joint-venture strategic alliance with a 900-person Japanese firm with which it conducts R&D.

Insofar as automation components feature in every facet of manufacturing worldwide, the automation industry is highly competitive. Over the past decade, Canadian manufacturers across the board have strived to reduce costs and increase profits. As a result, many companies have invested in automation equipment to boost the efficiency of their operations—a reality upon which Humphrey has capitalized.

Ten years ago, Humphrey's industry was dominated by North American manufacturers; today, Humphrey also faces strong competition from the Pacific Rim and Europe. In addition, its business is affected by the ups and downs of its customers, especially the Canadian automotive market, and the spillover of the semiconductor market into Canada.

Humphrey stays competitive through strategic partnering with its distributors and customers. Gone are the days when a salesperson could simply drop off a catalogue and wait for customers to call. Today, distributors and Humphrey design engineers work directly with customers, from an application's conceptual phase through to its after-market maintenance. Humphrey's well-educated staff, which includes graduates in Fluid Power Technology, gives the company a decided edge.

To heighten its customer responsiveness, Humphrey formed DaVinci Engineering in 1993. In this department, customers with specific problems—or unique applications—can receive the added service of a package designed specifically for them.

Another key to Humphrey's success is its partnerships with suppliers. In addition to its Japanese alliance, Humphrey Fluid Power Limited also cultivates key relationships in the U.S. and Germany. Through these strategic alliances, Humphrey's Canadian customers can buy many pneumatic and automation products from one source, thus lowering administrative and service costs. In return, Humphrey provides information about the Canadian market, enlightening its foreign partners about products that are then developed for the North American market.

In the future, Humphrey Canada expects the continuation of a trend that favours the growth of the manufacturing sector versus that of the resource sector. Over the long term, Humphrey's outlook is promising, thanks to improved governmental support for manufacturing.

In 1999, Humphrey plans to upgrade its office space and warehouse, and add more technically trained staff. When it does, it will certainly remain in Markham, where a reasonable tax rate, strong workforce, and solid base of technologically advancing companies have served the company well.

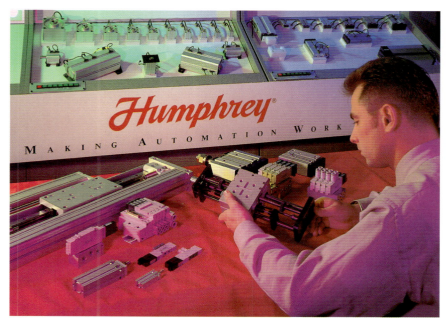

Customers can visit Humphrey's Automation Technology Centre for a hands-on opportunity to learn about the company's pneumatic products and services.

At the Automation Technology Centre, customers can learn about Humphrey's motion control and pneumatic products through individual static displays and moving models.

Delfour Corporation is a world leader in the development of information technology systems for the third party and contract logistics industry. Delfour's advanced information products and applications improve the effectiveness of warehousing processes with unique applications and solutions that made it a pioneer in the industry. The use of Relational Database Management Systems and the recent move to Java technology enables Delfour to maintain its leading role

Delfour Corporation

Delfour's state-of-the-art facility is expanding globally from its headquarters in Markham.

Technical support is provided 24 hours a day, 7 days a week.

in the production and implementation of logistics systems. Proprietary software meticulously tracks the progress of shipped products and manages the receipt of inventory. Clients now track manufactured goods from plant departure, through transit, to arrival at distribution centers and shipment to multiple points. Many other software companies have already adopted the unique features developed by Delfour to improve their own applications.

A wide range of companies in many industries now benefit from Delfour's leading-edge technology. Delfour's third-party logistics clients include many prominent shippers such as Federal Express, Ryder Integrated Logistics and Burnham Services. The market continues to grow rapidly as companies worldwide seek to outsource their logistics challenges. Delfour also enjoys high demand for information systems from other sectors. World leaders in high technology, telecommunications, food, hazardous goods, automotive components, pulp and paper, household goods and heavy equipment now store and ship their products through many of Delfour's clients.

Delfour logistics solutions are driven by customers' processes and requirements, an approach that distinguishes the company from its competitors. Systems have been designed to meet the specific needs and procedures of each organization and can handle multiple facilities and multiple customers simultaneously, in contrast to competitors' products that typically require a different system for each facility.

The looming Year 2000 computer crisis is an obstacle in the paths of many companies, but Delfour sees it as an open road to opportunity. This ominous event has increased the demand for replacement systems. Delfour is already prepared to satisfy this demand with advanced system solutions.

Future plans include development of auxiliary tools that will be integrated into its line of products and services. The facility to determine profit margins by customer will soon become a standard feature of Delfour systems. Joe Couto, president of Delfour Corporation, says, "Determining profit margin by customer and applying Activity Based Costing methods won't be unique to our systems alone, but doing it well will be."

Visitors are always welcome at Delfour Corporation.

Several Web-enabled applications will soon be launched. Internet-based programs will allow Delfour clients to offer their customers access to essential information on-line. As a result, existing private networks will be replaced with networks that are much more efficient and less expensive.

Delfour also plans to expand its role in supply-chain management by integrating Delfour applications with supply chain management applications that manage the entire life of a product from inception to arrival at the customer's door. States Couto, "Looking to the future, we will ensure a deeper involvement in the flow for the best possible business performance."

Delfour was formed by a group of professionals who understand warehousing and logistics. They provided consulting and software-related services to North American warehousing organizations before founding Delfour in 1988. The company is expanding globally from its headquarters in Markham, Ontario, and now has offices and employees in the United States, Brazil, Argentina and the United Kingdom. Delfour has recently extended its reach to Chile and Mexico. Client Falabella operates Chile's largest department store and is also a partner with Home Depot in that country. In Mexico, Transportacion Maritima Mexicana (TMM), one of the country's largest logistics providers, now employs Delfour's technology to operate the port of Acapulco.

Delfour relocated its corporate offices to Markham because of the competitive tax rates and beautiful landscape populated by Canada's most prominent high-tech companies.

All Delfour clients receive in-depth training.

Computron Systems Inc. knows about good things coming in small packages. That's because rather than spreading itself across the landscape of computer products and peripherals, this Markham, Ontario-based company concentrates on the select neighbourhood of notebook computers.

Established in 1987, Computron has grown to become a specialised distributor of

Computron Systems

HyperData notebooks across Canada, marketing through resellers, dealers, and value-added resellers. In addition, it assembles notebooks in its new 15,000-square-foot facility, which it has occupied since December 1997. Computron also handles Original Equipment Manufacturer business for larger companies in the market for their own brand of notebooks. And if companies require parts for notebooks, Computron will source them.

Amin Rhemtulla, president and founder of Computron, believes his company's edge lies in the modular nature of its products. Unlike other major companies, Computron builds computers to meet the needs of its buyers. The flexibility provided by a customised notebook is of great advantage to clients. For example, if a client plans to use a notebook solely for word processing, Computron can build it without the cost of advanced features. However, if the notebook is to be used for heavy graphics work, Computron can build it with a large viewing surface plus all the latest features. With a HyperData system presentation possibilities are virtually unlimited. And convenient, too, with an infrared mouse!

Currently, Rhemtulla and his 30-person company are thriving within a growing niche as more users choose notebooks over desktop replacements. Indeed, some universities now require that students bring computers to lectures.

These days, Rhemtulla says, notebooks are meeting the challenge of changing requirements. Increasingly, their capabilities equal or surpass those of the anchored desktops. Meanwhile the price barrier that once kept these convenient alternatives out of reach is falling. "Soon," he predicts," everyone will have a notebook."

Computron's new and expanded home in Markham, Ontartio.

Presently, Computron's products are manufactured under ISO 9001 certification, and the Markham facility is completing the process for ISO 9002 certification. This certification will lend demonstrable proof to Computron's commitment to a high standard of business practices, integrity, and reliability. Because of its roots as a service company, Computron clients have come to depend on excellent after-sales support which sets the company apart from its competitors.

To more efficiently meet the needs of clients, all service is performed in-house by factory trained technicians. Clients receive professional technical support through a toll-free phone number. Computron's sales staff supports its clients by offering product training, joint sales calls, and product demonstrations.

In the near future, Rhemtulla plans to further his company's service department. Until recently, Computron has only serviced its own HyperData brand products. Now, the company will service all notebook brands, filling a void in the marketplace. This eye to the future has been and will continue to be the reason for Computron's rise to prominence in the competitive computer industry.

Computron's technical service centre, where notebooks are assembled to meet clients' needs.

If employees of Markham, Ontario-based InSystems Technologies Inc. happen to forget what their employer is all about, they can simply flip over their business card to read the company's mission statement. "InSystems develops and markets innovative software solutions that make organizations more successful by redefining the way they create and manage their business document assets."

InSystems Technologies

Or they could check with Michael Egan, president of this computer software firm, who stays in touch with his 130 employees by taking new staff to lunch, making appointments to "reconnect" with long-timers and employing an "open-door" policy.

A fast-rising software-industry star, InSystems does most of its work with financial services organizations, which use the company's knowledge-based document-processing software to produce complex documents such as insurance policies, contracts, sales proposals and customer statements. InSystems works with more than 170 customers in 14 countries. The majority are U.S.-based, but the company is also aggressively pursuing opportunities in Europe and Australia. InSystems' PC-based desktop software has helped clients increase productivity by as much as 500 per cent, while significantly decreasing operating costs.

In 1996, InSystems received a $4-million injection of venture capital, which enabled it to invest significantly in R&D, sales, marketing and customer support. Currently, Egan says, the company's biggest challenge is coping with rapid growth: in a recent 15-month period, InSystems tripled its staff, and it expects to continue to double its sales as it has for the past four years, until it reaches its $100-million goal in 2001.

When InSystems opened its doors in 1989, it launched a product called Mosaic, which has been its workhorse through the 1990s. The company also acquired another product, Tracker, which enables U.S. insurance customers to fully automate their compliance filing process.

InSystems staff take pride in assisting customers before, during and after a sale, from analyzing the client's business needs to implementing the software and measuring its success. Most customers take advantage of the company's ongoing professional services, including training and consulting.

InSystems is pursuing new markets through alliances with systems integrators and independent software vendors. Its ultimate vision? To become the world leader in enterprise document processing, a goal which will involve the continued development of leading-edge document assembly, document management workflow and Internet-based technologies.

Michael Egan, president of InSystems Technologies Inc., employs a strictly "open door" policy at his 130-person software solutions company.

A rootin', tootin' desert hoedown highlighted a recent InSystems User Conference in Scottsdale, Arizona.

Shaping a Destiny 89

Eprom Inc.

Computer hardware distributor Eprom Inc. had operated from an office in Scarborough, Ontario since its inception in 1985. In 1997, the company relocated to Markham, Ontario, the hub of the computer distribution industry. Managing Director Paul Ling reasoned that "when you are not competitive, you move away from your competitors, but when you want to be competitive, you want to be where your competition is."

Today, Eprom and its staff of 55 occupy 25,000 square feet of office, warehouse and assembly space where they custom build computers, sell parts for PC compatibles and service a range of computer products. The company also has an office in Hong Kong where it sources its products.

Eprom currently sells through dealers and consultants from its office but Ling says the company is planning to open up more distribution channels across Canada in order to gain additional market share. Customers for its Power Link brand name personal computer systems include individuals, businesses and governments.

Operating in a highly competitive computer industry, Ling stresses the importance of finding a market niche. For example, when multimedia products became a computer industry phenomenon in the mid 1990s, Eprom was one of the first companies to enter into the new field. Eprom ultimately built its reputation on CD-ROMs, CD titles and sound cards. Although multimedia has now become a mainstream commodity, customers are able to remember Eprom for its groundbreaking work in the field and associate the company name with excellence in multimedia products.

Eprom Inc. and its 55 employees occupy 2,250 square metres of office, assembly and warehouse space in Markham, Ontario.

Eprom has increasingly begun to focus on building custom systems, in part due to the slimming of margins of multimedia products. In order to further this business, the company has obtained CSA certification on its systems and is applying for ISO 9002 status. "I believe that all future business with large corporate customers, schools and governments will require that the computer systems that they purchase are CSA and ISO certified," Ling explained. "If our systems do not have these designations, we will lose business to our competitor who has the certifications."

Ling described today's computer industry as a "very stressful" place to make a living. It is crucial to keep up with changing technology and new products. In addition, he added that a strong supplier today may not be one tomorrow, resulting in the continuous effort of seeking new suppliers for its products. Ling admits that it is a tough business, but being vigilant is critical to the survival of the company.

With offices in Markham, Ontario, and Hong Kong, Eprom Inc. custom builds computers, sells parts for PC compatibles and services a wide range of computer products.

"Once your products become commodities, you are not going to make it," Ling said. "You must keep evolving with technology, and be able to offer new products to your customers. If you are stuck with a product for a month, you have lost money. You have to be really sharp."

It was 1983, William Tong, a Canadian-trained electronic engineer who specialized in switching power supply technologies, foresaw the potential growth and influence the PC would have on the way people conduct their daily business. Tong determined to fill the need for an AC-to-DC power supply unit that surpassed the quality and safety requirements of that time, and pioneered the design and manufacturing of switching power supplies specifically for the PC industry.

Jaba System Inc.

Jaba became the first Canadian company to be awarded the seal of approval from CSA on the power supply unit as a standard computer component, which the company sells to resellers, industrial and government accounts.

Since then, Jaba has advanced along the trail Tong blazed nearly two decades ago, and has gone well beyond the traditional AC-to-DC power supply units, which it continues to manufacture through its affiliate offshore.

Today, with Jaba's 18,000-square-foot ISO-9002 registered Markham head office, annual revenues exceeding $16 million, an in-house design and engineering team to support original equipment/design manufacturing (OEM/ODM), and an industry that knows no boundaries, Tong has expanded his business even further. Jaba's line-up now includes a full spectrum of PC based components; customize computer systems through private label and built-to-order programs; and a full line of DC-to-DC power supply units marketed under the Sunpower brand name, which comes in various form factors and ranges from 15 to 1200 watts, designed and engineered specifically for industrial applications.

Clients also rely on Jaba to provide a total solution on the effective deployment of business computers and the implementation of networking methodology. "As we move towards the next millenium, computer and telephone systems will become more closely integrated," says Tong. "In this area, Jaba is forging new territories with our Computer-Telephony-Integration (CTI) solution. We're always on the leading edge of technology," Tong further states. "This technology will be the ideal alternative over traditional implementation and deployment methods of telephone and computer services, because it provides a more cost-effective means of deploying a hybrid telephone/computer system for large call centres or businesses that require an interface between their database/application software and telephone switching systems."

"The company is fully Canadian owned, with an ISO-9002 designation, groundbreaking CTI products, and specializes in DC-to-DC power supply units," says Tong, emphasizing, "Jaba has a distinct competitive edge."

Leading-edge products coupled with a thorough knowledge of the global marketplace, has resulted in exponential growth for this Markham-based company in both its domestic and export market. Furthermore, strategic alliances formed with leading manufacturers such as 3Com, Altigen, Appro, Compaq, Hewlett Packard, Intel and Microsoft have allowed Jaba to obtain insights into the latest technological development and product trends in the global marketplace. "Being privy to such first-hand information, and our pursuance on product excellence, has enabled us to position ourselves one step ahead of the competition, providing our business partners worldwide with quality products and innovative solutions for their computing needs," Tong concludes.

Jaba's founder, Mr. William Tong, customizes the design of a power supply unit for an OEM customer.

Jaba's head office is located in Markham.

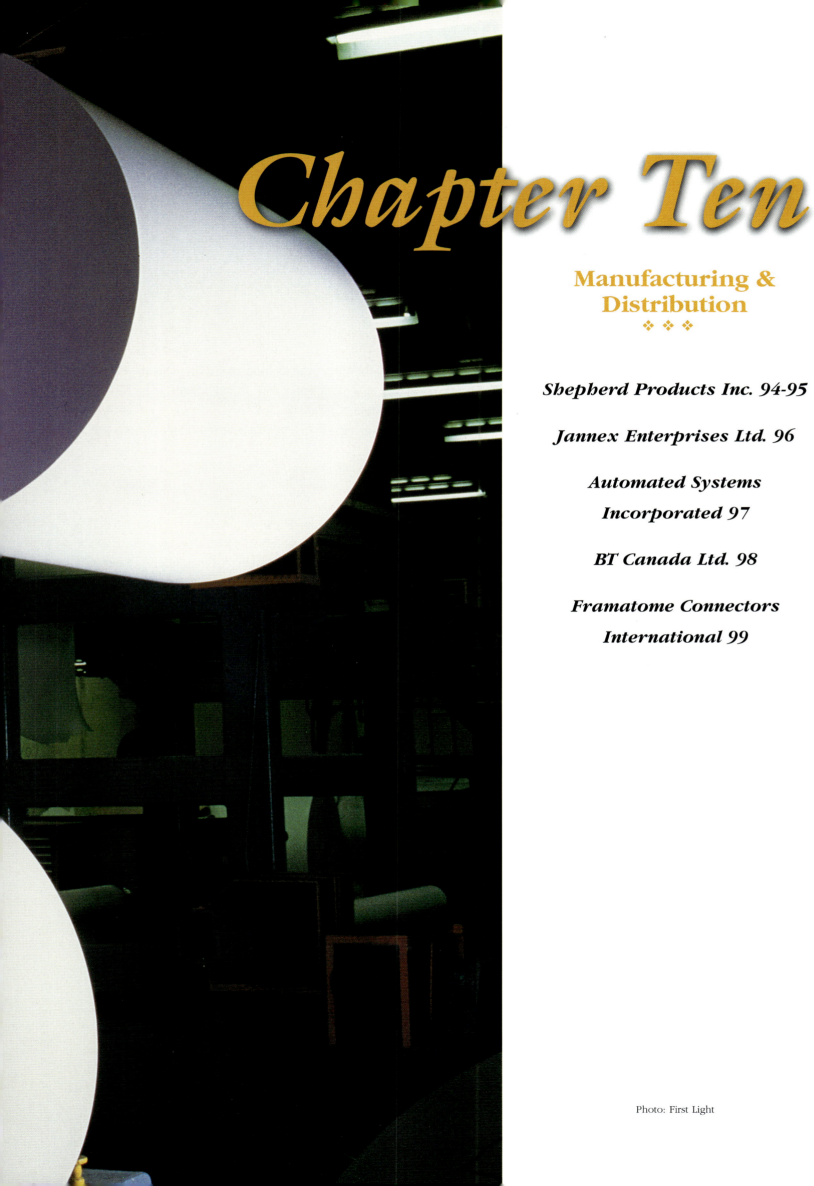

Chapter Ten

Manufacturing & Distribution
❖ ❖ ❖

Shepherd Products Inc. 94-95

Jannex Enterprises Ltd. 96

Automated Systems Incorporated 97

BT Canada Ltd. 98

Framatome Connectors International 99

Photo: First Light

Founded in the United States in 1956, Shepherd Products Inc. is owned by the Chicago-based Marmon Group of companies, a privately owned empire of industrial manufacturing enterprises with 27,000 employees worldwide. Shepherd Products began operations in Leaside, Ontario in 1957, and then moved to Markham in 1970 to become an independent Canadian operation, which employs 300 at the 165,000-square-foot facility. Recently, Shepherd

Shepherd Products Inc.

opened a new 48,000-square-foot manufacturing facility in Gallatin, Tennessee.

Shepherd Products began as a manufacturer of metal ball furniture casters and evolved into an unlikely range of products, to include TV stands and charcoal grills. At one time, Shepherd was North America's largest manufacturer of gas barbecues.

In the mid-1980s, the company focused on plastics. At that time, plastic was making headway in a market previously dominated by aluminum and wood. Shepherd introduced plastic twin-wheel casters mainly directed at the office seating industry. Next came the launch of plastic chair bases to the North American market, beginning with one style and size and expanding to a dozen. Over the years, the chair industry has shifted towards five-legged bases, which provide more stability than four-legged bases, thanks largely to the introduction of plastic. Chairs have also changed from those made with wooden seats and backs to plastic seats with plastic backs, and as a result of this change, it has made chairs less expensive for the consumer and more adaptable to ergonomic forms for the manufacturer.

Shepherd Products Inc. employs 300 at the 165,000-square-foot facility in Markham, Ontario.

In the 1990s, the company extended its plastics line into a complete line of chair components to include seats, backs, arms, column covers, casters and bases. From a logistics standpoint, plastic products are preferable because they are lightweight. From a design point of view, colours are inherently moulded into the part, so there is no paint to peel and they can be colour-matched to upholstery.

Markham gives the company a steady labour force and good resources, along with excellent transportation routes. Shepherd's major market is expanding more rapidly in the United States than in Canada. The southern United States is a major growth area in the seating industry.

Shepherd plans an expansion program that will see the size of its Markham facility increase by 30 per cent. They have grown substantially over the past seven or eight years. Today, Shepherd has the most complete line of any North American manufacturer. They are without a doubt "the leader in plastic chair components."

Beginning as a manufacturer of metal-ball furniture casters, Shepherd now produces plastic twin-wheel casters in various sizes and styles.

Thanks to Shepherd Products, the introduction of plastic bases has provided more stability for office seating.

Shepherd ships up to 60 per cent of its products to the United States, Mexico and South America. Currently, the company is considering setting up manufacturing operations in other parts of the world, including Europe and Asia, where local firms present the strongest competition.

But what distinguishes Shepherd from its competition is not only the products it sells, but also its service and quality. With a large emphasis on research and development, Shepherd stays ahead with new designs and products, most of them patented worldwide. The company has representation strategically placed in each major growth area in Canada, the United States, Mexico and South America. The on-time delivery record is outstanding, and customer service is second to none in the industry.

In the 1990s, Shepherd Products has extended its plastics line into a full range of chair components to include seats, backs, arms, column covers, casters and bases.

Shaping a Destiny 95

Surrounded with tasteful greeting cards of every size and type, the 2,250-square-metre showroom of Jannex Enterprises (1980) Limited promises hours of delightful shopping to find the perfect sentiment for that special person.

In addition to greeting cards, the Markham, Ontario-based company imports and distributes calendars, stationery, gift wrap, social memory books, gifts for impulse buying, art cards and posters. The company sources products worldwide

Jannex Enterprises Ltd.

and represents them on an exclusive basis for distribution in Canada through gift and card shops, art galleries, museum shops, book stores and selected department stores.

Under the watchful eyes of Charlie Chaplin and "company mascot" Punzi, Jannex principals Ellen Bean and David Hes examine new products with Adam Hes, the company's customer service manager.

Jannex principals David Hes and Ellen Bean, the company's president and vice-president, respectively, embrace a sales philosophy that emphasizes high-end quality: both in product value and customer service. The 35-person corporation strives to treat everyone, both inside and outside the company, as a customer. This includes not only clients and suppliers, but also each other.

Unlike its competition, Jannex employs its own salespeople in the populated areas. Where other companies engage agents, who may represent several competing lines, Jannex staff are dedicated to their own company. As a result, Jannex believes it can offer superior results to its suppliers, superior service to its clients, and superior benefits to its staff.

Due to the activities of U.S.-based companies, Canada's greeting-card industry is growing more and more competitive. Often, suppliers look to a company like Jannex to build the Canadian market for its products, then launch their own sales program once the market is proven. As a result, Jannex continues to explore opportunities to represent more European products.

Before adding a new product to its line, Jannex looks for production value, uniqueness and artistic quality. But its main goal is to stay on the cutting edge with products that even avant-garde art galleries and museum shops haven't seen before.

Like the business of high fashion, however, the greeting-card industry depends on changing style. Images on cards, gift wrap and stationery are all fashion statements: if green is the color of the day in interior design or on the Paris runways, for example, green also will dominate the shelves of paper products. Even subject matter can be in or out. Cases in point: Jannex's now-popular cigar-theme calendars and cow-theme stationery.

Among the company's current offerings are compact disks packaged in designer tins. These canned collectibles, featuring the music of Glenn Miller, Franz Schubert and Edith Piaf, to name a few, are an international effort: the disks are pressed in England and Germany; the tins are designed in Germany and Italy. But none other than Jannex enjoys the exclusive right to sell these distinctive products in Canada.

Iwona de Xavier, purchasing manager, and Adam Hes, customer service manager, discuss a product in the Jannex showroom.

Everybody has seen photos of huge equipment sliding off the assembly line—but how many people stop to consider the manufacturing efforts behind the assembly line itself? At Automated Systems Incorporated, that's all they think about.

Founded in 1985, Markham, Ontario-based ASI builds automated assembly equipment, principally for the automobile industry. It equips "first-tier" suppliers—

Automated Systems Incorporated

companies that make everything from door hinges to fuel-level sensors—with the means of production to deliver their own products to last-stop assemblers.

Because its assembly lines are complex, the company builds each one in modules. Each "work cell" is responsible for a particular function along the line. Each cell connects seamlessly with those on either side of it, yet remains an independent unit. Each section has its own electrical panel, which can be swiftly disconnected from its neighbor and linked to any new addition that a manufacturer wishes to make.

Through the years, ASI has kept its equipment consistent; as a result, a unit purchased today will match up readily with a manufacturer's existing equipment. This improves the ease of maintenance of ASI products, makes life easier for operators with little time to master new equipment and enables the stocking of uniform spare parts.

In addition to such versatility, ASI credits its success to excellence in machine design and focused customer service for putting it ahead of its competitors in this specialized field.

ASI's 50 employees are quick to say they're proud of their work—and it shows: in late 1997, the Markham Board of Trade recognized ASI with a first-place award for Entrepreneurship and Innovation. It shows in the high customer satisfaction that has led to a lot of new business as a result of word of mouth.

For the future, ASI's primary goal is to keep its impressive growth trajectory on course. Indeed, since 1993, ASI has tripled its sales, and has a strategic and aggressive plan in place to target specific markets and customers.

Currently, ASI serves clients in Canada, the United States, Mexico, the United Kingdom and South Korea. ASI plans to increase its worldwide presence, and company executives are confident that their choice of home base will facilitate that goal. The abundance of high-tech industry in Markham makes sourcing parts and information much easier. And, because ASI ships much of its product by truck, its location at the intersection of many major highways is fortuitous.

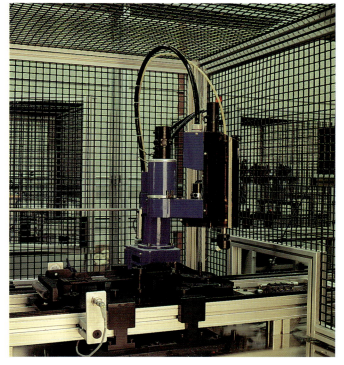

Increasingly, state-of-the-art assembly lines built by Automated Systems Inc. include robotic stations.

Automated Systems Inc. is a leading manufacturer of automated assembly lines, particularly for the automotive industry.

BT Canada Ltd. is behind—and beneath—the success of much of the world's business. Literally.

That's because the Markham, Ontario-based company sells internal material-handling equipment, including hand and powered pallet trucks, stackers and reach trucks, to customers in the distribution, storage, retail and manufacturing industries.

BT Canada Ltd.

As a seller of internal material-handling equipment, Markham, Ontario-based BT Canada Ltd. is behind—and, literally, beneath—the success of much of the world's business.

BT Canada provides hand and powered pallet trucks, stackers and reach trucks to customers in the distribution, storage, retail and manufacturing industries.

In addition, the company uses proprietary software to analyze customers' needs and design appropriate solutions. It also sells parts, services its equipment and offers short-term equipment rentals.

The company's $600-million Swedish parent, BT Industries, was formed in 1945. Worldwide, BT Industries has 14 subsidiaries and distributes products in more than 100 countries. In Canada, the company has been in existence since 1975.

Like most businesses, BT Canada operates in a highly competitive environment. Because its products are based on European designs, BT Canada markets on the basis of features and benefits—such as ergonomics and compactness—rather than price.

While BT Canada's products are 25 to 30 per cent more expensive than those of local competitors, the total costs of the equipment over its useful life are often less, says President Paul Bennett.

"Sometimes, the smallest outlay in a product's lifetime is the initial purchase price," he says. "You might pay more for our product up front, but over its lifetime—8 to 12 years, depending upon application—if there are fewer repetitive strain injuries, if the operator is more comfortable and, thus, more productive, well, you do the math."

Over time, BT Canada has progressed from selling simple hand pallet trucks to becoming a force in the internal forklift industry. In Europe, BT has about 20 per cent of the internal forklift market; in Canada, its market share is 12 per cent, but more than twice that in Ontario.

From the beginning, 55-person BT Canada has been headquartered in Markham. "It's very much on the leading edge of technology," Bennett says. "We've got good access to major highways, both across the city and north-south. And, it may sound trite, but it's a nice place to live and work."

Recently, BT Industries AB completed a $500-million acquisition of its largest North American competitor. In addition, the company continues to develop its program of national accounts. Over the past three years, BT Canada's nine salespeople have secured numerous large accounts, particularly in the grocery industry.

If you're looking to get connected, Framatome Connectors International is the place to start.

Framatome Connectors International is respected worldwide for its leadership in connector technology. In North and South America, Europe and the Asia Pacific, FCI serves customers through five business groups dedicated to meeting the unique challenges of each of its market industries—namely, data processing,

Framatome Connectors International

telecommunications, consumer electronics, controls and instrumentation, electrical power and construction, industrial equipment, aerospace, military and automotive.

With sales networks and a total of 44 manufacturing facilities in more than 20 countries, FCI possesses the infrastructure necessary to support more markets than any of its competitors, anywhere in the world. What's more, it can offer a wider range of interconnection systems, including application tooling, than any other company.

FCI enjoys this powerful point of differentiation not only because of its size, but also because of its dedication to understanding customer needs. From reading market trends to asking questions—and listening to the answers—for guidance in the quest for technological innovation, FCI leads its industry. The company's focus on global research and development and quality management at all levels are other valuable tools for anticipating and meeting customer needs. Equally important are the more than 8,500 people who power the company, enabling it to be a technological force on a global scale.

The 65,000-square-foot FCI Automotive Markham manufacturing facility is located on Renfrew Drive.

At the heart of the company is FCI Automotive, which supplies terminals, connectors and interconnection systems for any automotive application including wiring harnesses and equipment, printed circuits and fibre optics. FCI Automotive also system designs and produces custom insert-moulded products for electronic, electrical and electro-mechanical applications.

With 14 locations and 2,100 employees worldwide dedicated to serving the automotive industry, FCI Automotive can always be found near its customers. This strategic arrangement enables FCI Automotive to offer high levels of customer, sales and technical support. In addition, the division can react quickly to customer needs by shortening lead times and cutting costs.

State-of-the-art assembly automation for insert moulding and airbag connector product lines

FCI Automotive is a relative newcomer to Markham, Ontario, having opened its manufacturing centre in 1993. Since then, the company has established a presence of considerable impact. Indeed, product sales have quadrupled, and employment has grown to more than 100 from just 20.

As worldwide demand for connector systems continues to expand, FCI Automotive anticipates being an integral part of this dynamic industry—and of the Markham business community—for years to come.

Bibliography

Champion, Isabel. *1793 Markham 1900*. Markham District Historical Society, 1989.

Champion, Mary B. *Markham Remembered*. Markham District Historical Society, 1988.

A History 200 Years Yonge. Regional Municipality of York, 1997.

Moving to and Around the Greater Toronto Area. Toronto: Moving Publications Ltd., 1996.

The Reesor Family in Canada. Published by the Reesor family, 1980.

Acknowledgements

The author also gratefully acknowledges the following sources of information:

Chinese Cultural Centre of Greater Toronto
Department of Economic Development, Town of Markham
Department of Recreation and Culture, Town of Markham
Frederick Horsman Varley Art Gallery of Markham
Information Markham
Markham Board of Trade
Markham Chinese Baptist Church
Markham Guild of Village Crafts
Markham Museum and Heritage Village
Markham Theatre for Performing Arts
Markham Stouffville Hospital and Participation House
Milne Outdoor Education Centre
North Toronto Historical Society
Richmond Hill & Markham Business Association
Scarborough York Region Chinese Business Association
Seneca College of Applied Arts and Technology
Shouldice Hospital
Toronto Buttonville Municipal Airport
York Region Catholic District Board of Education
York Region District Board of Education
York Technology Association

Enterprise Index

Automated Systems Incorporated 97

BridgeStreet Accommodations 72

BT Canada Ltd. 98

Ceridian Canada Ltd. 69

Computron Systems 88

Comtronic Computers 80

Craig Riley's Markville Lincoln Mercury 66-67

Delfour Corporation 86-87

Eprom Inc. 90

Framatome Connectors International 99

GE Multilin 82-83

Humphrey Fluid Power Limited 84-85

IBM Canada Ltd. 78-79

InSystems Technologies 89

Jaba System Inc. 91

Jannex Enterprises Ltd. 96

JJ Barnicke Limited 74

Markham Board of Trade 64-65

Shepherd Products Inc. 94-95

TD Financial Group 68

Technica House Canada Inc. 81

Toronto Airways Ltd. 75

Town of Markham 70-71

V.V. DeMarco Properties, Limited 73

Index

A

Ace Hardware, 30
Adult Basic Literacy program, 58
Allstate, 30-31, 51
Almira, 13, 20
American Express, 30
Angus Glen Golf & Country Club, 35, 52
Apple Canada Inc., 15, 30, 38-39, 44
Applefest, 52
Army Medical Corps, 13
Arts York program, 51
ATI Technologies Incorporated, 38
Automated Systems Incorporated, 97

B

Bailey bridge, 14
Bank of East Asia (Canada), 44
Bell, 50-51
Bayview Avenue, 46-47, 57
Berczy, William, 11-12
Big Blue, 39
Bishop, Billy, 14
Box Grove, 20
Briarwood Farms, 20
BridgeStreet Accommodations, 72
British American Cultivator, 12
BT Canada Ltd., 98
Buttonville, 13, 30, 34

C

Cachet Centre, 32
Canac Kitchens, 31
Canada's National Research Council, 39
Canadian Field Artillery, 13
Canadian Mounted Rifles, 13-14
Canadian National Railway, 14, 34
Canadian Pacific Railway, 34, 46-47
Canadian Technology Network, 39
Carlton Road, 49
Cedar Grove, 15, 20
Cerebral Palsy Parent Council of Toronto, 56
Ceridian Canada Ltd., 69
Chait, Stephen, 38
Cham Shan Temple, 45-46
Chan, Yolanda, 45
Charlie Pilksticker Leadership Award, 59
Cherkas, Andy, 59
Cheseborough-Ponds (Canada) Inc., 31
Chinese Bowling Congress, 44
Chinese Community Centre of Ontario, 46
Chinese Cultural Centre of Greater Toronto, 47
Church Street, 57
Commerce Gate, 32
Communicator,, the, 47
Communities in Bloom, 24
Community Gardens Project, 52
Computron Systems, 88
Comtronic Computers, 80
Confederation of Greater Toronto
Consumers Gas, 51
corduroy roads, 12
Cornell, 22-23
County of York Directory, 12
Cousens, Don, 40
Craig Riley's Markville Lincoln Mercury, 66-67
CyberTrends Inc., 38

D

Delfour Corporation, 86-87
Denison Street, 47
Dickinson Hill, 13, 20, 23
Digital Equipment, 30
Digital Processing Systems, 39
dirty thirties, 14
Duffin's Creek, 19
Dundas Street, 45

E

Eckhardt, Salem, 49
Emerson Electric Canada Ltd., 31
Eprom Inc., 90

F

First Markham Place, 32
Ford Electronics Manufacturing Corporation, 30, 38
Forrester, Maureen, 51
Fortino Mall, 47
Fortune 500 companies, 30
407 ETR, 32, 34
Framatome Connectors International, 99
Frederick Horsman Varley Art Gallery, 21, 49-50

G

Gaidatsis, Helen, 59
Galleria, the, 31-32
GE Multilin, 82-83
General Electric, 30
German Mills, 12, 25
German Settlers Park, 52
Glynnwood Retirement Residence, 57
GO Train, 24, 34-35
Goldense International, 46
Golf Digest, 52
Good News newsletter, 24
Great War, the, 14
Greater Toronto Area (GTA), 28-31, 34, 46, 52
Gristmill Marketing, 23
Group of Seven, 21, 49-50, 59

H

Heritage Festival, 52
Heritage Schoolhouse, 57, 60
High-Tech Business Directory, 24
Highway 7, 20, 50, 56
Highway 48, 13, 24, 52
Highway 404, 20
Highway 407, 24
Honeywell Bull Limited, 40
Hong Kong Money, 46
Hughes, Dean, 20
Hughes, D. Evelyn, 20
Humphrey Fluid Power Limited, 84-85
Hurricane Hazel, 14-15

I

IBM Canada Ltd., 15, 30-31, 37-41, 51, 78-79
Industrial Mentorship Program, 59
InSystems Technologies, 89
International Economic Alliance, 31
Iroquois, 11

J

Jaba System Inc., 91
Jannex Enterprises Ltd., 96
JJ Barnicke Limited, 74

102 Shaping A Destiny

Johnson & Johnson, 30, 38
Johnson Controls Limited, 38
Joint Board Consortium, 58
Joint Declaration, United Kingdom and China, 46

K

Kathleen Gormley McKay Art Centre, 49, 53
Kennedy Avenue, 24
Kiefer, Robert, 31

L

Laine, Cleo, 51
Lake Simcoe Conservation Authority, 58
Langstaff, James L., 12-13
Langstaff, Lillian, 13
Langstaff, Rolph, 13
Laval, Quebec, 35
Law Development Group, 22
Lee, Ivy, 43-44, 47
LEGO, 31
Lester B. Pearson International Airport, 34, 39
Lister, Avril, 22
Little Rouge River, 19
Locust Hill, 20, 24

M

macadam road, township's first, 12
Main Street, 15, 49
Market Village, 24, 45
Markham, William, 11
Markham and Scarborough Plank Company, 12
Markham Board of Trade, 7, 31, 64-65
Markham Chinese Baptist Church, 45
Markham Civic Centre, 32, 52
Markham Concert Band, 51
Markham District High School, 57, 59
Markham Economist, 13
Markham Fair, 14, 20, 26-27
Markham Fair Grounds, 14
Markham Guild of Village Crafts, 52
Markham Heritage Estates, 23
Markham Little Theatre, 51
Markham Men of Harmony, 51
Markham Mobility Bus, 57, 59
Markham Museum, 13, 17, 23, 51-52
Markham Neighbourhood Support Centre, 57
Markham Pathways Project, 52
Markham Physiotherapy Clinic, 57
Markham Road, 13
Markham Sun, 13
Markham Stouffville Hospital, 22, 31, 55-56, 59
Markham Theatre for Performing Arts, 50-51
Markham Township, 14
Markham Village, 13-15, 20, 23-24, 57
Markham Village Grammar School, 57
Markham Youth Theatre, 51
Markham's Small Business Self-Help Office, 40
Markhaven Incorporated, 57
McAlister, Mark, 40-41
McKay, Kathleen Gormley, 49, 53
Metropolitan Radial Railway, 13
Military Service Act, 14
Mill Road, 12
Milliken Mills, 20, 22-24
Milne Dam, 13
Milne Dam Conservation Park, 52
Milne Park, 24
Milne Pond, 24
Mitsubishi Electric Sales Canada Incorporated, 38
Model Community Demonstration Project, 35
Modesty magazine, 43, 47
Morine, Robert, 30
Morris, Julie Wang, 47
Motorola, 58-59
Mound, Ashley, 58

N

NCR, 51
New China Bookstore (Canada) Ltd., 47
Nike, 30
The Nylons, 50

O

Oak Ridges Moraine, 19
Oakville, Ontario, 29
Office Depot, 30
Ontario Marketing Awards, 1997, 24
Ontario Simcoe and Huron Railway, 13
Ontario Waste Minimization Award, 35

P

Pacific Mall, 24, 32, 44, 46-47
Participation House, 56, 59
Peters, Tom, 56
Petticoat Creek, 19
Pickering, Ontario, 11, 13, 20
Pillsbury, 31
Pioneer, 31
Polygram, 31
Pomona Mills bridge, 14
Pomona Mills Park, 52
Pomona Plank Road, 12
Prime Minister's Award for Teaching Excellence, 59

Q

Quaker Oats, 30
Quebec Railway, 13
Quinn, Mike, 41

R

Recycling Council of Ontario, award, 35
Richmond Hill, Ontario, 12-13, 20, 29
Richmond Hill-Markham Chinese Business Association, 44-45
Robotics Championship, 58
Rompin' Ronnie Hawkins, 50
Roth, Barbara, 53
Rouge River, 12-14, 24
Royal Bank, 51
Royal Flying Corps, 14

S

Scarborough-York Region Chinese Business Association, 31, 45, 47
Scott, David, 51
Second Canadian Field Regiment, 14
Second World War, 14, 20, 46, 56
Shark's Fin City, 44
Shepherd Products Inc., 94-95
Shouldice, Edward Earle, 56
Silicon Valley North, 7, 37, 39, 41
Simcoe, John Graves, 11
Sing Pao Daily News, 47
Sing Tao, 47
Society of Bubbleology Club, 59
Spadina Avenue, 45
Steelcase Canada, 31
Steeles Avenue, 23
Stirling Douglas Group, 38
Stouffville, Ontario, 13
Sun Microsystems, 30
Synervoice, 38

T

Take Our Kids to Work, 59
TD Financial Group, 51, 68
Technica House Canada Inc., 81
Thorne, Benjamin, 10

Thornhill, 12, 14, 20, 23, 30, 53, 55-57
Timex, 31
Toogood Pond, 20, 52
Toronto, Ontario, 9, 12, 14-15, 24, 29, 31-32, 34-35, 39-41, 44-47, 59
Toronto Airways Ltd., 75
Toronto and Nipissing Railway, 13
Toronto Buttonville Municipal Airport, 32, 34, 39, 75
Toronto Cathay Lion's Club, 44
Toronto Chinese Golf Association, 44
Toronto Star, 59
Toshiba, 31
Town of Markham, 7, 52-53, 70-71
Twiddy, Carl, 59

U

Unico Bridge Fair, 58
Unionville, Ontario, 12-16, 20-24, 29, 49, 51-53, 58-59
Unionville Festival, 22
Unionville Golf Centre, 52
Unionville High School, 51, 58-59
Unionville Theatre Company, 51
United Kingdom, 11, 44, 46
United Way of York Region, 57
Urban Frontier, 52
Uxbridge, Ontario, 13

V

Valleywood Drive, 45
Varley, Fred, 21
Vaughan, Ontario, 23
Victoria Cross, the, 14
Victoria Park Avenue, 37
Victoria Square, 20
Volunteer Action Fund, 30
V.V. DeMarco Properties, Limited., 73

W

Wan, Tony, 47
Warden Avenue, 50
War of 1812, 12
waste management, 35
Whitchurch, Ontario, 13
William Berczy Public School, 58-59
Wong, Kit, 44-45
Woodbine Avenue, 47
World Journal, 47

Y

Yonge Street, 11-13, 15, 23
York Central Hospital, 12-13
York Region, 31, 51-52, 56-58
York Region Board of Education's Partnership Award, 58
York Region Catholic District School Board, 57-58
York Region District Health Council, 57
York Region District School Board, 57-58
York Region Food Network, 52
York Symphony Orchestra, 51
York Technology Association, 40-41